2th EDITION

FOOD TRUCK BUSINESS

First Published in the United States of America in 2018

FOOD TRUCK BUSINESS

2 Books in 1

COMPLETE GUIDE FOR BEGINNERS, LEARN THE FOOD TRUCK BUSINESS STRATEGIES TO INCREASE YOUR SALES AND TURN YOUR PASSION INTO FINANCIAL SUCCESS

RYAN BOURDAIN

DONALD MURPHY

TABLE OF CONTENTS

FOOD TRUCK BUSINESS GUIDE FOR BEGINNERS 10

INTRODUCTION 11

CHAPTER 1: GOOD REASONS TO OPEN A FOOD TRUCK....................15

FOOD TRUCKS...16

WHY FOOD TRUCKS?..17

RISE OF THE FOOD TRUCK ENTREPRENEUR 17

THE RIGHT ATTITUDE...18

WHAT IT'S LIKE 18

FINANCIAL GAINS..19

A POTENTIAL FOR PROFIT 19

PITFALLS OF FOOD TRUCK OWNERSHIP.....................................19

Lack of Planning 20

Doing Everything Yourself..20

Poor Service..22

Ignoring Budgeting..23

Poor Marketing 24

OTHER OPTIONS..25

Food Carts 25

Concession Stands 26

Kiosks and Booths..26

Gourmet Trucks 27

Bustaurants...27

CHAPTER 2: ALL ABOUT THE COSTS OF STARTING A FOOD TRUCK........29

SELECTING THE RIGHT FOOD TRUCK? NOT ALL FOOD TRUCKS ARE THE SAME! 31

CHAPTER 3: WHERE CAN YOU FIND A FOOD TRUCK IF YOU WANT TO START YOUR OWN BUSINESS? 34

WHERE TO FIND FOOD TRUCKS FOR SALE...................................36

SEARCHING NATIONWIDE 37

CHAPTER 4: WHAT ARE THE BEST SOURCES OF FINANCING 47

DEBT FINANCING 47

PERSONAL FINANCING 49

EQUITY FINANCING 49

OTHER 50

CHAPTER 5: GETTING LICENSES AND PERMITS FOR YOUR FOOD TRUCK
....**51**

SPECIALIZED INSURANCE FOR THE FOOD STREET VENDOR AND FOOD TRUCK.......53

Food Street Vendor..53

Food Serving Truck 54

NEW YORK FOOD TRUCKS FOR HAPPY EATING 54

CHAPTER 6: STRATEGIES AND MENU IDEAS **56**

PLAN YOUR MENU..56

PRICING YOUR MENU...60

EXTRAS..65

CHAPTER 7: THE MOST INTEGRAL FACTORS OF STARTING A FOOD TRUCK BUSINESS..**66**

IS THE MARKET SATURATED?..66

Testing The Market 67

Research on the Success of Food Trucks like Yours 68

Try a Formal or Informal Survey....................................68

"Dry" Runs..69

Creating the Brand 69

RESEARCH FOOD VENDING IN YOUR AREA 81

WHY IS MY STATE DIFFERENT THAN THAT STATE?.........................84

CHAPTER 8: PLANNING FOR THE FOOD TRUCK BUSINESS OPERATIONS 86

OFF TRUCK KITCHENS AND COMMISSARIES 86

Inventory And Maintenance 87

MANAGING OPERATIONS 87

Food Preparation and Procedure 87

Labor and Personnel..88

Planning for Long Term Growth......................................88

Document Management..88

Supplies...89

SAFETY 90

Protect yourself...90

Emergency Plan...91

CHAPTER 9: BUILD YOUR TEAM **92**

HIRING 92

FIRING...93

HUMAN RESOURCES 94
CHOOSE YOUR VENDORS 94
BRANDING 94

CHAPTER 10: GETTING READY FOR INSPECTION 97
THE PURPOSE OF HEALTH INSPECTORS 97
TYPES OF INSPECTIONS 98
BASIC INSPECTION GUIDELINES 99
Commercial Kitchen or Commissary 99
Good Food Practices 100
Food Safety Knowledge 101
SAMPLE FOOD INSPECTION 103

CHAPTER 11: MISSION, VISION, AND GOALS 106

CONCLUSION 109

FOOD TRUCK BUSINESS STRATEGIES 112

INTRODUCTION 113

CHAPTER 1: WHO STOPS AT FOOD CARTS? 116
THE FREEDOM TO MOVE 117

CHAPTER 2: WHAT IS CHEAPER TO RUN, A RESTAURANT, OR A FOOD TRUCK? 119
PROS OF FOOD TRUCKING 121
CONS OF FOOD TRUCKING 122

CHAPTER 3: DRAFTING THE BUSINESS PLAN 123
WHAT IS A BUSINESS PLAN AND WHY IS IT REQUIRED? 123
POINTS TO PONDER IN THE PLANNING OF FOOD TRUCK BUSINESS 124
The Local Food Truck Marketplace 124
Understanding the Competition 125
BUSINESS STRATEGY 125
Cost Leadership Strategy 125
Differentiation Strategy 126
Location Strategy 126
Hybrid Strategy 127
FOOD PRICING 127
USE OF STRATEGIC PARTNERSHIPS 128

CHAPTER 4: FINANCIAL PLANNING 130
WHAT NUMBERS SHOULD I KNOW? 130

HOW CAN I CREATE NEXTGEN NUMBERS?...132
HOW DO I INCREASE MY PROFIT?...135
CREATING THE PROFIT FORECAST 139
COMPILING ALL EXPENSES 139
MONTHLY EXPENSE FORECASTING TOOL..140
DETERMINING CAPITAL REQUIREMENT 141
ACCEPT CREDIT CARDS ANYWHERE..142

CHAPTER 5: EXPENSES AND CASH FLOW **144**
OPERATING EXPENSES 145
MANAGING FOOD VOLUME 145
BUILDING LOYAL CUSTOMERS..146

CHAPTER 6: MARKETING STRATEGIES AND PRICES, PROMOTIONS, ETC.
....**148**
OFFER SOMETHING FOR FREE..148
LET THE ORDER LINE BE LONGER THAN THE PICKUP LINE............................149
OFFER ITEMS FROM YOUR CATERING MENU..149
ALWAYS ASK IF THEY WOULD LIKE A DRINK 150
ADVERTISE YOUR MENU ON SOCIAL MEDIA 151
MAKE SURE THE SPOT'S WORTH IT 152
Food Truck Parking During Business Hours..................................158
Food Truck Parking During Off Hours...158
Event Parking 158
TOOLS OF TRADE: WEB SITE, CARDS, STATIONERY 159
So Much Digital Media, So Little Time...159
Social Media...160

CHAPTER 7: LAUNCHING AND POST-LAUNCHING TIPS TO KEEP THE
FOOD TRUCK RUNNING **164**
TIPS TO SUSTAIN THE SUCCESSFUL RUN AFTER SETTING UP 165
Feel free to market yourself..165
Think freely and do not attach yourself to an idea 166
Expand on the revenue streams...166
Be open to teaming up 166
Keep networking 166
Make a good investment in your staff..167
Put a good price tag on your food items 167
FOOD SAFETY..167
How to Get Smart About Food Safety?...168
Why Must I Use Commercial Equipment? 169

Some Basics About Food Safety 170
MAINTAINING YOUR FOOD TRUCK IN THE WINTER 171
Ensure your normal upkeep is up to date 171
Take a look at your antifreeze.. 171
Check your tires.. 172
Review and replace your wipers.. 172
Watch out for your windshield washer liquid 172
Proceed with your yearly upkeep as necessary, in addition to your
winter maintenance 172
SUCCESSFUL FOOD TRUCK MARKETING 173
Food truck occasions! 173
Putting resources into your very own Branding. 173
Your name reveals everything.. 174
Ensure your truck is appealing. 174
Train your staff to have astounding customer service. 174
QUALITIES THAT A FOOD TRUCK VENDOR MUST HAVE 174
Patience 175
Innovator 175
Friendly 175
Creative.. 175
Time Management 176

CHAPTER 8: FALSE ASSUMPTIONS ABOUT OWNING A SMALL BUSINESS
....**177**
MYTH #1: RELYING ON OTHERS FOR ANSWERS AND INFORMATION BLINDLY..... 178
MYTH #2: THERE ARE FREE GRANTS AND BANKS THAT WILL LOAN INDIVIDUALS
MONEY IF THEY ARE STARTING A BUSINESS 178
MYTH #3: PEOPLE WILL AUTOMATICALLY LOVE AND KNOW ABOUT YOUR BUSINESS
WHEN YOU OFFICIALLY LAUNCH... 179
MYTH #4: BEING RESISTANT TO THE NOTION THAT YOUR ORIGINAL BUSINESS IDEA
AND CONCEPT WILL CHANGE AND EVOLVE 180
MYTH #5: THERE IS ONE SET MAGIC FORMULA FOR EVERYONE WHO WANTS TO
START A BUSINESS 180

CHAPTER 9: HOW TO KEEP A BUSINESS HEALTHY IN THE LONG RUN..182
WHAT ELSE DO YOU NEED?.. 182
HOW ARE YOU PREPARING TO ADJUST SO YOU CAN MEET THOSE TRENDS? 183
PLAN FOR THE MOST EXCEEDINGLY TERRIBLE 184
DEVELOP SOLID RELATIONSHIPS.. 185
CHECK-IN, ASSESS, AND CHANGE AS YOU PUSH AHEAD 185

CHAPTER 10: HOW DO I CREATE PROFITABLE AND PREDICTABLE PROCESSES..**186**

CAN YOU FRANCHISE A FOOD TRUCK? 188

CHAPTER 11: FOOD TRUCK BUSINESS SUCCESS TIPS **191**

GET CREATIVE WITH YOUR SAUCES...191

PLAN THE WORK, WORK THE PLAN 192

TRACKING YOUR PROGRESS 195

Keep Track of What You Sell *195*

Keep Track of Your Costs...*196*

Keep Track of the Day's Revenue *197*

Take as Many Pictures as Possible *197*

Have Pictures of Your Food Visible *198*

Let People Know Your Location.......................................*199*

Prep as Much as Possible Before Arriving.......................*200*

Test Your Food Before You Sell It....................................*201*

Have a Tip Jar...*201*

Clean the Truck at The Day's End *202*

CONCLUSION..**203**

FOOD TRUCK BUSINESS GUIDE FOR BEGINNERS

A STEP BY STEP GUIDE ON HOW TO START A MOBILE FOOD BUSINESS AND WORK TOWARDS MAKING IT SUSTAINABLE AND PROFITABLE

RYAN BOURDAIN

DONALD MURPHY

Introduction

The mobile food industry is continually soaring to new heights. If you haven't yet seen a food truck in your city, you will soon see! When a food truck shows up in a neighborhood, it drives hordes of people to exit their homes and offices to sample unique and delicious foods. Even the traditional food booths at festivals are starting to be replaced by food trucks. What could possibly be the reason? When a food truck is around, people tend to know that there'll be tasty foods to be found.

While chowing down on some of their favorite meals, a lot of patrons are noticing the incredible income potential of owning a food truck. Today, more and more people are seeing this as an entrepreneurial opportunity. This has led many of the same patrons to leave their boring jobs for one that offers excitement and new challenges every day! Others, who have dreamed of opening a restaurant, have now seen a lower barrier to entering the food truck business thus making their dreams easier to achieve.

Many people who start food trucks come from the corporate world with backgrounds in marketing, sales, public relations, real estate, and more. They take their business skills and pair it up with their love for food. Often times, they eventually get to create a new source of sustainable income. Some of the youngest food truck owners haven't even received their diplomas from college but their entrepreneurial spirit has driven them into launching a business that can continue to run long after they've graduated. Food trucks in many ways seem like an overnight sensation. Selling food on the street has been around for ages. Ice cream trucks and hotdog stands are nothing new but the real fun has come from a new twist on an old concept. In recent years, food trucks have gone from selling fries, hotdogs, and ice cream, to becoming something else entirely.

Fresh and exciting paint jobs are combined with innovative and creative new food types are now served off trucks, and their popularity is no doubt expanding. A lot of people (me included), have looked to this new market as a possible business venture for themselves. What's not to love? You get to set your own hours, your own prices, make your own food, control what you sell, and reap the rewards; all the while having fun serving food on the streets. Whether you're a chef with many years of experience or someone who wants to take a crack at being an entrepreneur, food trucks are a great way to run a kitchen and manage a business.

Unfortunately, it's not always as easy and as profitable as it may appear. If you've seen the movie "Chef" (and you should see it because is a nice movie), it may seem like long lines are always just waiting for you to pull up and open your truck window. Within a few weeks, Chef's truck had people lining up around the block just to get a taste of what he was cooking. After the first few weeks on my truck, I can tell you that the lines weren't that long (nowhere near).

Owning and operating a food truck business for the past two years has taught me a lot of lessons, most of which aren't necessarily skills you've already learned in the kitchen or in a business course. This book is meant to prevent current and aspiring food truck owners from making simple yet costly mistakes, as well as showing how it's easy to make a profit if you follow a few simple guidelines and stay on top of certain key details. It is not meant to be a book on how to make an awesome double cheeseburger, or how to master double-entry accounting. In short, this book's intention is not to teach you how to cook awesome food types, or how to run a small business, it is meant to teach you how to run your food truck business more successfully, while avoiding some of the mistakes that a lot of people make when first starting out. All the methods listed are meant to help you:

- Get repeat business

- Keep losses to a minimum

- Avoid first-timer mistakes

- Satisfy customers

- Maximize profits

A lot of tips listed here are things that may seem very common, but are nonetheless important. In a lot of instances, the most common sense things can slip our minds and leave us with unhappy customers or a bottom line in the red, also known as NO PROFIT.

It's easy to just focus on what you love to do; cook food, or run a business. It's the smaller things, however, that can often mean the difference between making money and losing money, and if you're just starting out, it will be crucial to not only be consistently making money but to avoid those big losses that can cost you a lot in the long run.

By the end of this book you'll be able to:

- Avoid costly and embarrassing mistakes that often arise on a food truck business

- Increase your chances of long-term street service success

- Distinguish yourself from other trucks

All of these tips are the things that I have learned that are critical to having success on the street, and are things that I wish I could have avoided or taken advantage of, from the very first time. That is why I wrote this book; so that you could learn from my mistakes and avoid them as a beginner thus increasing your odds of immediate success in the food truck business, and paving the way for a long-lasting, profitable business.

Why do I feel qualified to write a book on running a successful food truck? Well, for one, I've been at it for two years. They've been two hard and difficult years in a lot of ways, but also are the years I had most of the fun, cooking and working. For me, in a lot of circumstances, I was simply winging it and going with what I thought was best at the time.

Looking back on it, there were lots of benefits from figuring things out on my own, but there were also a lot of avoidable costs. Learn from a few of my failures and successes, and I believe this book will prove to be worth much more than what it costs.

This book is designed to inspire and introduce you to the fascinating world of the food truck industry. It is for men, women, students, dads, moms, and anyone else who has been mesmerized by the popularity of food trucks. Like starting any business, it's going to take a lot of work but it can change your life! Let's get ready to explore the different aspects of what it takes to start your own food truck!

CHAPTER 1:

Good Reasons to Open a Food Truck

Starting a business is a dream many of us have! Imagine being your own boss and setting your own hours. You could be making money for yourself and eliminating the long commutes, and the unsatisfying and unrewarding job. If the idea of working for you sounds appealing, then the food truck industry might be what you're looking for! The food truck industry is growing at an enormous rate and part of that growth is due to the slow economy.

Just about every city in North America has been hit by the gourmet food truck revolution and it appears that it has come to stay. Every month, new trucks are being launched from coast to coast. At the end of 2011, the industry-tracking-website *"Mobile-Cuisine.com"*, estimated that at least 10 new trucks a month were hitting the streets. That number is much higher now. These new food trucks specialize in gourmet-style food with unique twists. Forget about the standard hot dogs, burgers, and tacos. So boring! These trucks have reinvented classic dishes and more, into gourmet versions that rivals menus from the best restaurants!

Food Trucks

One way of avoiding falling into the restaurant trap is to open a food truck. You've probably seen these everywhere by now. They're takeaway places that operate from the back of a truck, literally. Park them anywhere, serve food, and drive away into the sunset loaded with cash. Reality is a bit different, but the food truck business is booming in America. People are demanding great food with easy access more than ever. The rise of social media has led to cool food concepts gaining traction really quickly. While some of these influencers take advantage of businesses, food trucks don't have such issues. First of all, the concept of a food truck is cool enough to draw passers-by, Secondly, it is not as if some influencers can simply walk through your food truck and pretend to have eaten there. It's not a restaurant where one can order a glass of water and walk away, after all.

Food trucks offer customers convenience in that, they can pick their food up and eat it wherever they want. They don't need to wait for close to an hour at a sit-down restaurant or have to stand in lines to eat greasy food at fast food joints. The quality of a restaurant combined with the convenience of fast food is what makes food trucks such a compelling offer.

Best of all, the economics of a food truck business are a lot simpler to understand for beginners, as I'll be showing you in this book. I'll be taking you from the very first step of why you need a food truck business, to marketing, business plan writing, location scouting, and choosing a good truck.

The most intimidating part of a food truck business is getting approvals. Dealing with the government is always a headache, but in this book, you're going to discover that it's a lot simpler than you might think. Besides, there are more important things for you to take care of.

Thinking like a business owner is of paramount importance, but unfortunately most people have no idea what this means. To clarify, it doesn't mean that'll you simply chase money all over the place and cut costs indiscriminately. That's what someone who knows nothing about business thinks it is all about. Being a business owner is all about taking responsibility and accepting that your being in charge, is the best possible thing that could have happened to you.

Why Food Trucks?

Now it is important to understand why the food truck industry is growing so rapidly. A major part of this growth is a direct result of the poor economy and people losing their jobs. This has led numerous individuals to find new sources of income or even start their own businesses. Consumers are also growing more health conscious so, they're looking for healthy alternatives when it comes to food. A growing number of trucks are starting to cater for this audience by offering gluten-free and paleo-based dishes while more trucks have started to offer healthy alternatives, which is not the norm. Come to think of it, a cheese-stuffed burger with fried bacon and a glazed donut for the bun is not exactly something a health-conscious consumer would order!

This huge growth can also be attributed to significantly lower start-up costs than a brick-and-mortar restaurant. This is one of the key motivating factors for starting a food truck. These rolling kitchens can also be relocated easily if the business is slow and requires less staff to operate. On the other side of the industry are the customers. Good food always attracts people! And when it's good, they love to share their eating experiences. That's because a large part of our social gatherings is based around food. With this basic understanding of people and business, it's clear that the mobile food industry can offer some incredible opportunities for creative entrepreneurs!

Rise of the Food Truck Entrepreneur

So how is it that there are so many entrepreneurs launching new food trucks each and every month? Some have chosen to become entrepreneurs by choice. Others have been thrown into a desperate situation by factors out of their direct control. Everyone has a different reason for starting a food truck. Oftentimes, a food truck is used to expand an existing business (like a restaurant or a catering company), or it's a way to create a second income stream for individuals.

Others have started food trucks because they are unemployed or have lost their jobs for one reason or another. More adventurous individuals usually start a food truck because they just want to try something different. They'll actually quit their day jobs to try their hand at running a food truck business full-time. Even well-known food businesses are starting to notice the potential in the mobile food industry. For instance, Jack in the Box, Chipotle, Whole Foods, and other well-known national restaurant chains and stores, have started their own food trucks to capitalize on their share from this industry.

Even with so many newcomers, the food truck industry continues to grow at an alarming rate! It's a great way to get into the foodservice business where you can be rewarded for your hard work while gaining the appreciation you deserve!

The Right Attitude

The type of service rendered could be the make-it-or-break-it part of this business. Introverts who cannot push themselves (or who are not willing to push themselves) to be more outgoing, are not meant for this type of business and should therefore look for other means of earning cash. It is vital to establish this early on to make sure that no time, effort, or money will be wasted.

What It's Like

Delving into this type of business may require some major modifications to the lifestyle as it is fast-paced and requires multitasking. It is also very physically demanding and requires a hands-on effort of the owner. Some of these physical efforts include carrying heavy objects such as buckets of ice, the ingredients, coolers, generators, the cart itself, and many more. However, since there will always be a demand for food and because hot dogs are almost considered a metropolitan delicacy, there is only a low level of risk with this type of business.

Although there is less work involved in this type of job compared to other lines of work, the hourly wage is considerably higher. All it takes is the right business plan and a tasty product for a sufficient amount of money to be earned, even on the first day of operation.

Financial Gains

As an example, starting up a hot dog cart does not require big capital. The startup cost may range anywhere around $ 2,000 to $ 10,000 and this is already inclusive of the cart, materials to be used, business permits, and other fees required to comply with some legalities.

Many hot dog vendors attest to being able to earn around $ 200 to $ 500 in a day with just one cart. If the statistics remain constant and if the vendor will sell his or her goods on a daily basis, the proceeds will amount to around $ 6,000 to $ 15,000 in a 30 day period.

Just imagine how much the earnings would be if, in due time, the business expands and more carts could be put out. In fact, an article in the Wall Street Journal stipulated that several successful hot dog operators can round up annual earnings of $100,000 or more.

Moreover, if the vendor decides to cater to some events, the sales for that day will be doubled or even tripled, depending on the marketing strategy used and how smooth the sales may go. On big occasions, such as local festivals, Mardi Gras, or even sporting events, some vendors earn around $ 1,500 to $ 3,000 by the end of the day.

A Potential for Profit

This is huge as food trucks hold great potential for profit. All it takes is proper management skills and the right strategy.

Pitfalls of Food Truck Ownership

I've listed the advantages but there are some pitfalls you need to be aware of. I don't mean to present food truck ownership as the key to great success. The truth is that it takes a lot of work. You'll need to execute a lot of processes well and constantly evaluate how your business is doing. Many food truck owners get lazy after achieving initial success and this proves to be their downfall. Here are some of the other pitfalls to beware of.

Lack of Planning

There are a few items you'll need to plan before you get your business up and running. Chief among these is your business plan. Your business plan outlines everything that is relevant to your food truck operation. It lists what your locations will look like, what kinds of customers you'll target, and other financial information. Most importantly, it'll also outline when you can expect to make your money back.

This is a crucial point to consider when starting any business. You cannot run a business without capital, and too many business owners fail to consider their true costs. They assume their ventures will be successful from the first day but this is never the case. It takes around six months to a year for your cash flow to stabilize. You need to account for these low sales periods and have enough cash in the bank to pay your bills and maintain your standards.

Without proper planning, you're unlikely to be able to project any of this. Planning is tedious and it isn't exciting. But I'm going to show you how to turn this thought process on its head and make planning, something you look forward to. Always remember: "If you fail to plan, you plan to fail".

Doing Everything Yourself

Most business owners tend to love having control. However, most business owners also fail. The successful ones learn to let go of their need to control everything and learn to delegate and provide clear instructions to their employees and to the people assisting them in their business. The average person has a warped view of the tasks a business owner carries out.

Common wisdom says that a business owner needs to wear many hats. They need to understand their business, understand operations, understand marketing, figure out taxes and accounting, and also make time to pay themselves. The mistake occurs when the common person thinks that a business owner needs to execute all of these things by themselves. There's a difference between wearing a hat and being a full-blown professional at everything.

As a business owner you need to understand whatever is relevant to your business, in each of those fields. You're not a superhero and aren't perfect, no matter what your dog thinks of you. You cannot hope to become an expert in all of those areas instead, you need to focus on what you're good at, and consult with those who know what they're talking about when you need to deal with the other stuff. For example, if you're seriously considering opening a food truck business (since you're reading this book I'm assuming you are), you're probably well versed in cooking food and understand how to present your cuisine. Let's assume you don't know a thing about marketing, legalities, accounting, setting up a business structure, or even how to run a kitchen. Here's the good news: You don't need to know all of this. What you need to do instead, is learn whatever you can and outsource the tasks that you cannot comprehend. Hire an accountant and use their services to open your business and file your taxes. Hire a junior cook to help you in the kitchen, and talk to or observe other food truck owners to see how they run their operations. If you're deficient in marketing, hire a great graphic designer to create logos and marketing material for you. Have someone create a great website for you, and then also hire a freelancer to incorporate a location tracker.

Whatever you need, there's help for it. The internet has made it so easy for you to find the right people so much so that all you need to do is click a button. So let go of the need to understand everything about everything. Even Michelin's starred chefs hire pastry chefs to prepare desserts. Do you think they sit down and prepare their accounts themselves? Do they fix their plumbing issues themselves? They can't even prepare their food by themselves; they need an army of chefs to do so. So let go of the need to control everything, and instead focus on your strengths. Outsource the rest and success will follow.

Poor Service

You won't have to deal with front-of-house operations when running a food truck, but this doesn't mean you can ignore customer service. To be a successful business, you need to listen to your customers and give them what they want. This is a tough pill to swallow for a lot of restaurant and food service business owners. Why is this? Let's call it the artistic temperament. Everyone has ideas of what food should taste like and what works best. You might think that salt is overrated and might refuse to add any to your food. However, if the majority of your customers prefer tons of salt in their food, who are you to argue? A famous chef can get away with kicking out customers who want to change the way their food is cooked, but you can't.

This doesn't mean you need to compromise your ideals or serve unhealthy food. However, you need to strike a balance between your artistic side and the health of your business. Compromise is necessary, and you need to remind yourself of why you're running a business. Be passionate about the food you cook and be equally passionate about running a good business. You're probably not the only one who depends on its health. There are no tables to clean or water to serve so this makes customer service quite simple. The typical food truck customer wants food quickly, and served fresh and tasty. They want their food cooked right and served with a smile. These aren't tough things to do for any business owner. Have fun running your business and your customers will have a great experience as well. Don't compromise the quality of your food or your cooking to make more money. In the short-term, you will make money, but in the long-term your customers will recognize the drop in quality and will visit some other business. Make sure your food stays fresh and delicious. In the interest of saving time, many food truck owners (and restaurants) cook food beforehand and freeze it. This robs food of its texture and taste. Reheating food in the microwave is no one's idea of cooking.

This is where planning comes in handy. If your menu is elaborate and is full of food that cannot be reasonably prepped beforehand and cooked at short notice, you'll need to change your menu. A food truck customer isn't going to wait for more than five minutes for their food. The idea is to deliver great taste, quickly and conveniently. Tailor your menu to achieve this and your customers will always be happy.

Ignoring Budgeting

This is a mistake you think most business owners would avoid, but it's alarmingly nonetheless. Many business owners fail to keep track of their receipts and merely guess how much money they're making. It's usually a loss so there's nothing to report there. If you're someone who doesn't keep track of spending and budgeting in your personal life, then forget about opening a business right now. You're not going to magically start budgeting once you open a business.

You'll only replicate what you do in your personal life. If this involves zero tracking, or very loose tracking, you're headed for trouble. A business isn't a game that you should take lightly. You need to be on top of everything. This isn't as hard as it seems, but it requires you to establish processes and consistently practice them.

For example, it should be standard practice for you to deposit the day's take, into your business bank account at the end of the day. Much like how kitchens need to be cleaned after the end of the day's service, you need to perform some financial tasks as well. At the end of every month, you need to take stock of how well you did and to plan for the future. You might need to invest more in improvements or on marketing to grow your business.

Cash flow is a challenge for every business owner. You never know when a crisis might occur, either in your own life or with the general economy, and you need to prepare buffers against these. Look at how badly small businesses have been wrecked thanks to the COVID-19 pandemic. It exposed just how unprepared most business owners were. I'm not saying they ought to have predicted how bad the pandemic would get. But, they should have held reserves of cash to prepare for the unexpected.

Just as you save for a rainy day, your business needs emergency cash on hand as well. The rule of thumb in personal finance is to <u>save six months-worth of expenses as cash</u>. Carrying this over to your small business accounts is an intelligent move and will give you a good margin of safety. Make tracking finances a priority if it isn't already one. Also make sure you incorporate good habits into your personal life. Carry these over to your business and you'll avoid falling into a debt hole.

<u>Poor Marketing</u>

You cannot rely on the old marketing adage that says; "Build it, and they will come"." That's not how marketing works. You need to consciously advertise and target your customers. These days, thanks to advances in digital marketing, it's possible to laser-target your customers. You need to get to know them beforehand (not personally, but their habits), and target them accordingly.

Any business that still relies solely on advertising in print media, and hopes word-of-mouth spreads, is preparing to fail. Your social media strategy needs to be robust. You don't need to keep posting every hour of the day, but you do need to remain active. If social media posting scares you, consider hiring someone to manage your profiles. Many business owners do this and it's an example of how you can outsource the tasks that you don't enjoy.

Marketing is all important these days because many things are competing for your customer's attention. You don't need to scream and shout to be heard, but you do need to invest in marketing and brand creation. A lot of marketing terms will sound like nonsense to you and it's true that marketers can take themselves a little too seriously. This doesn't mean they're wrong, though. Educate yourself on marketing basics and invest in good branding materials. They'll help you stand out more. If any of this worries you, then just keep reading. You'll gain a good grounding in all of the necessary topics by the end of this book.

Other Options

A food truck isn't the only mobile method of selling food. There are other options available, and it's important for you to review them before you decide to go all-in with the food truck idea. Some of these options might suit you better.

Food Carts

You've definitely seen one of these. In the US, they're mostly associated with hot dog and sandwich vendors. This might lead you to think that's all they're good for, but they can be as versatile as you want them to be. In the developing world, where food trucks aren't as common, food carts are used to sell entire meals.

Some of the examples of meals sold are street snacks that can be quickly cooked in a wok, soup, and ramen bowls. All of these foods are in demand in the US as well, so it isn't as if you can't use one to draw attention. A standard food cart is made of aluminum and stainless steel. They're modular and can be used in different ways.

Their portable nature makes it easy to set them up anywhere and they're a lot easier to obtain permits for. City officials don't have any vehicle related concerns with them, unlike with food trucks, and their portability means that even more locations are accessible to them. Instead of parking at a designated spot, you can push your cart right up outside offices and you're guaranteed to attract a steady stream of visitors.

The downside is that you won't do as much business as a food truck will. Carts are smaller and there's only so much food you can handle. However, you can do what many food cart vendors do and recruit someone else to keep bringing you fresh supplies. You can store your supplies either at a designated spot in a vehicle or at your home.

Repurposing a food cart is also very simple. If you try to serve just breakfast food and find that it has no takers, then in the afternoon, all you'll need to do is slide a few panels and you can have a lunch cart. Around 3 PM, you can have a mid-afternoon-snack-cart, serving coffee. This functionality isn't present in a food truck. It's going to look a bit odd if you spot a food truck serving pancakes during the day, Vietnamese cuisine for lunch, and donuts with coffee in the afternoon.

The flip side is that your brand creation opportunities are low, and it's going to be tough to scale directly from a food cart to a bigger business. You can aim to save enough for a truck and build from there.

Concession Stands

These fixed restaurants serve great food and have low overheads. Their locations also ensure that their owners manage to make a good profit. Concession stands are usually associated with movie theaters, but the most profitable ones happen to exist in stadiums. Stadiums these days are fitted out to be used for various purposes. While multiple sports aren't played at the same venue, concerts, and conferences often take place within them.

This makes renting a concession stand during such times a great deal. They're an event-related business, so it's not as if you can rely on them throughout the year. However, if you're looking to earn side-income or test the waters, this is a great way to test your idea. Most concession stands sell junk food, and as people grow more health conscious, there's greater demand for better food.

You can sell healthy versions of local food to draw customers to you. While ethnic food might not be a major draw due to the temporary nature of such stands, it's something to consider.

Kiosks and Booths

These types of food vending locations can be permanent or mobile. Some areas have permanent spaces dedicated to kiosks. Street fairs tend to draw a number of people who frequent food kiosks and booths. You'll find many kiosks popping up near beaches and other leisure areas.

They're not exactly mobile, but at the same time, a food kiosk isn't a permanent structure either. They're usually prefabricated and you can apply your branding to them. Unlike a food cart, you can't switch

26 | P a g .

your branding out. For all intents and purposes, a food kiosk or stand is a food truck without wheels. They have the same appeal but lack the mobility of a truck.

The lack of mobility is replaced by the guarantee of a great location. They're typically leased by the city to operators and the locations always have some festival or occasion taking place that attracts people to them. If driving around or purchasing a vehicle doesn't appeal to you, this is a good option.

Gourmet Trucks

The average food truck is thought to sell cheap and delicious food but there are a growing number of gourmet food trucks. These trucks sell food that is priced even higher than restaurants and attract dedicated fan followings. In many cases, they're used by aspiring chefs to launch their careers.

Food trucks are a cool way to show off on social media, and this helps explain gourmet food truck popularity. Influencers rush to review these trucks, and as a result, if you're an aspiring chef or business owner, you can receive great reviews. There are an increasing number of food truck rallies where different food truck operators gather at a location and people flock to them. The ability to sample food from different trucks is what appeals to them, and this increases the business that the food trucks generate.

Bustaurants

This is a food truck on steroids. Why stick to a food truck when you can buy a bus and seat your customers within it? They're quite popular in Europe where public transport is used more often by people, and they recognize the appeal of converting a bus into a restaurant. In London, old double-decker buses are repurposed as cool restaurants, and they manage to deliver a unique dining experience.

While costs are higher, this is a niche that can be tapped in the US. People will naturally be attracted to a huge red bus that serves food since they've never seen it before. You will have to bear some pioneering pains with regards to permits but it might be worth it. The ability to seat people within your bus and to operate a takeaway as a food truck usually gives you two ways to appeal to your customers. You'll need wait-staff, but given the smaller size of the seating area, you won't have to deal with the hassles of a full-blown restaurant.

CHAPTER 2:

All About the Costs of Starting a Food Truck

Don't think that you just need to spend a few thousand on a food truck business; it's not that frugal of a business. There are many factors you have to think about before getting to a point where you can comfortably be sure about the amount of money you're putting into that same business because it will take quite a few funds to ensure that your food truck gets off to a great start.

So, what costs actually go into a food truck business? Well, that's simple to answer. One of the more interesting things to note about a food truck business is that much of the costs will be partially reserved for legal fees, specifically those associated with getting appropriate permits, insurance, and legal aid. And, some of those legalities are actually time-gated in some states, or in other words, require some time on a wait-list before receiving one. Can you guess what that particular legality involves? That's right; getting the *Mobile Food Vending Unit Permit* to actually operate your truck! Some of the costs also involve getting potential employees up to speed, too. Many food truck vendors have a hand or two to keep their business running smoothly, so that's something to keep in mind if you're planning on running a relatively large food truck business. Now, let's take a look at a cost breakdown for the average food truck business. These figures, paraphrased from a food truck resource, actually account for figures derived from the East Coast region of the United States, specifically (and naturally) New York City. So, if you're planning on starting a food truck on the East Coast, these figures are a pretty good estimate to use as a guideline if you're already anticipating the costs. All figures are estimates, East Coast, the USA

- Truck: $50,000 (covers the cost of purchase and basic retrofitting)

- Mobile Food Vending Unit Permit: $200 + potential wait-listing (may cost $15,000 if acquired through third parties)

- Commissary: $500 per month; expected to cost at least $6,000 per year

- General Liability Insurance, business: $3,500 to $4,000 per year

- Mobile Vendors License: About $100 (accounts for about $50 for classes and $50 for a 2-year license)

- Truck Insurance: About $2,000 to $3,000 per year (estimates point to $2,500 per year)

- Commercial Kitchen: About $2,000 to $5,000 per month (estimates point to an average of $36,000 per year)

- Employee Wages: About $16 per hour (estimates vary throughout the year)

- Workers Compensation: About $7,000 per year (accounts for 3 employees, may vary based on number of employees)

- Accountant: About $350 per month (accounts for about $4,200 per year)

- PR Professional: About $1,500 for about 3 months (accounts for at least $6,000 per year)

When you add up all of those costs, the total cost of running a food truck business rounds out to about $150,000 to $200,000 and, that's just taking the average cost into account. Still, a food truck business can be rewarding, and rewarding enough to make well enough profits to cover those spent costs.

Selecting the Right Food Truck? Not All Food Trucks are the same!

Not all food trucks are made the same, but they all pretty much serve the same purpose. Food trucks, in fact, are known for carrying the equipment needed to prepare, cook, store, and serve different types of foods. And, given that those basic functions are what define the 'food truck,' you shouldn't really look for something that's too complicated on your first venture as a food truck vendor.

Most traditional food trucks provide lunches, so they're naturally equipped with all the tools to prepare various lunch-worthy foods. Foods like sandwiches, tacos, burgers, and kebobs are some of the food truck staples that regularly find themselves on the menus of many food trucks. Besides those staples, many food truck vendors now carry many vegetarian and vegan options to provide a truly diverse food selection.

You're going to want a good food truck for two main reasons. The first reason involves the fact that food trucks are large enough to handle anything you throw at them, in terms of preparing and storing the food onboard. It just eliminates the trouble of dealing with a smaller food cart. The second involves the fact that food trucks are a lot simpler to manage on a daily basis.

There are actually two types of food trucks you should watch out for in the market:

Mobile Food Preparation Vehicle (MFPV): This truck allows you to prepare food on the truck after customers make their orders. Most customers do have to wait a while to get their order, though this truck type essentially allows you to prepare fresh meals on board.

Industrial Catering Vehicle (ICV): This vehicle is pretty straightforward in function. It's the type of food truck that simply sells prepackaged foods, and nothing else. This is probably the first food truck you'll have if you're passionate about the business.

Mobile food preparation vehicles naturally cost more than an industrial catering vehicle, thanks to the nature of their functions. To give you an idea, many MPFV food trucks are known to cost more than $30,000, depending on the condition. Industrial catering vehicles cost thousands of dollars less. New and/or custom MFPV vehicles are known to cost as much as $100,000.

PLATFORM	BENEFITS / NEGATIVES	
Truck	□ Less susceptible to inclement weather □ Plenty of surface area to advertise □ Extremely mobile □ Well equipped with full kitchen	□ Most expensive option □ May be restricted from parking at your residence due to city ordnances or neighborhood covenants □ Expense to renting overnight storage when not in use
Trailer	□ Moderately priced □ May be parked in your driveway □ Plenty of surface area to advertise □ Extremely mobile □ Equipped with adequate kitchen	□ Susceptible to inclement weather □ Will require a vehicle to tow
Tent	□ Least expensive option □ May be parked in your driveway inside a towable trailer	□ Most susceptible to inclement weather □ Requires additional components to advertise what you're selling □ Time consuming to setup and break down

You don't have to settle for a $100,000 food truck, though. There are many lower-priced options that can do just what you need to do. Long before you finalize your purchase of a food truck, you need to make sure all of your legalities are taken care of. What legalities do you mean? The legalities involved with getting the appropriate licenses and permits.

CHAPTER 3:

Where Can You Find A Food Truck If You Want To Start Your Own Business?

Now, you should be able to get your own truck for your business. You should be ready to shell out around $20,000 to $40,000 for this, plus you should also be ready to cough up some money for the equipment that you will be using.

If you feel like it's too expensive, don't fret. If you're really serious about this business, you have to be ready for all these expenses because you should have a truck that will meet the public health standards. As for the equipment, it always differs as it's based on your needs and preferences and on the kind of food business that you have. If you're planning to sell hotdogs, you should have all these frying equipment, as well as containers for the condiments and the other ingredients. If you're planning to sell pizza, you should have ovens, baking pans, trays, and the like. You can also save money if you're planning to just sell pre-packaged foods already, so mainly you just need to have a lot of containers around.

Also, it would be great if you decide which kind of food truck business you are going to embark on. This will help you decide which types of equipment you need, and will also help you when it comes to decorating your food truck based on your niche.

Here are some of the types of food trucks that you should know about:

1. **Mobile Food Preparation Vehicle:** This is a food truck that lets customers order their food and wait for their food to be cooked. Even though that's the case, it's also imperative that you should not let your customers wait for long. It's like your typical fast-food restaurant or a fast-food kiosk, so of course, you expect that your customers are already hungry. So it's best that you make them great food and serve them as soon as you can. They are also called concession trailers.

2. **Industrial Catering Vehicle:** As the name suggests, this is the kind of truck that you can take around towns, such as those old-school ice cream or hotdog trucks that you see around. Industrial catering vehicles mostly sell pre-packaged foods, which makes it more cost-friendly than a mobile food preparation vehicle. The only catch is that you have to make sure that you're able to sell everything right away or else you'd be throwing away a whole lot of cash because obviously, you can't sell what's already spoiled. Both industrial catering and mobile food preparation vehicles are often found in school fairs, concerts, and other events where there are loads of people around.

3. **Gourmet Food Trucks:** Imagine eating the best gourmet foods in an unusual setting; that's what gourmet food trucks are all about! Sometimes, you want to eat at a certain restaurant but you can't because you haven't got any reservations but with the presence of gourmet food trucks,

you'll be able to enjoy the food that you want as they sell specialty foods, such as velvet cupcakes, Korean barbecue, orzo fries, crepes, and even smoothies or other kinds of drinks that can't usually be bought outside. Of course, these food trucks require special equipment so you have to be ready for the fees, but if you already get to establish your name in the food truck industry and if you already have a following; it'll be easy for you to earn back your capital. Sometimes, you can also invite well-known chefs to cook for you, or if you're a chef yourself, this can be a good place for you to showcase your cooking prowess!

Decide which type of truck you'd like to use for your business then go on and plan your menu.

Where to Find Food Trucks for Sale

When you start your search for a vehicle, the first question that often comes to mind is where to find food trucks or step vans on sale? Obviously, the quickest and most convenient place to start is locally in your own town. Get to know some of the other food truck owners in your area and ask them where they found their truck. Food truck owners are usually happy to answer questions like this; however, they might be a little hesitant if the food truck you are going to operate competes directly with theirs. But in any case, getting the information straight from people who have already gone through the process is a great place to start. You can also call or visit local commercial vehicle dealerships to see what type of inventory they have on hand. In some cases, these dealerships are part of a bigger automotive network and can search their inventory in other regions where they do business. The advantage of going to a commercial vehicle dealership is that you can evaluate the vehicle immediately. Keep in mind that the used inventory can be sparse. Often, you'll find that the dealer inventory consists of used trucks that were delivery vehicles or other sorts of commercial utility vehicles that are not suitable for food trucks. But if you're fortunate enough to find a truck that has been previously converted to a food service vehicle, the time it takes for you to get it ready and operational can be dramatically minimized.

Of course, online options are plentiful when it comes to searching for a food truck. And chances are that you will be able to find a fully equipped food service vehicle online. Whether it's located near you is another story. Starting your search on your city's Craigslist site gives you the best chance of finding a vehicle locally. Often, you'll find private sellers that are either going out of business or who are selling their business to move onto other endeavors. You can sometimes find the best deals this way if the owners need to sell quickly.

Searching Nationwide

If you can't find any local vehicles that fit your needs, then you'll have to expand your search on websites that have listings for a wider region or even the whole country. The choices are definitely better but the disadvantage is that the vehicles are located further away and you can't easily evaluate them in person.

Here are some of the commercial vehicle sites where you can do additional research and find the available vehicles from around the country:

- CommercialTruckTrader.com

- TruckPaper.com

- TruckerToTrucker.com

- UsedVending.com

EBay is also a great place to conduct your research. You can find vehicles from both private and commercial sellers as well as get a good idea of the pricing for vehicles in different conditions and with different options.

There are also fully equipped trucks as well as base vehicles that need to be converted to a food truck. With any of the online options, you as the buyer will be responsible for all shipping and delivery charges unless you travel and drive the truck back to your hometown yourself.

Be sure you are familiar with driving a commercial vehicle and verify whether you'll need a commercial driver's license or not before you take the vehicle on the road.

Here are some things to check or verify when buying a used food truck or trailer.

- **Smells**

  ✓ What does it smell like inside? Greasy, sour, moldy, musty?

  ✓ Has it been smoked in?

  ✓ Air it out for 20 minutes while looking around and then smell it again. Non-food odors could be a serious problem requiring a serious time cleaning or replacing.

- **Windows**

  ✓ Open and close each window to make sure it aligns straight and latches tight when closed. Be sure it isn't too sticky.

  ✓ Check the condition of the wall and the flooring under the windows for soft spots indicating leaks.

- **Awnings**

  ✓ Is there a powered canvas awning?

  ✓ Where does the awning end?

  ✓ Test the awnings to ensure they work properly. A broken awning can be a $1,500 replacement cost.

  ✓ With the awning open, look at the fabric of the awning. Is it faded? Ripping? Starting to separate?

- **Serving Window Awnings**

  ✓ Do they fit inside the frame properly?

  ✓ How are they locked?

  ✓ Does it stay up or slowly start to close?

  ✓ Leave the window cover awning up while you inspect the rest of the vehicle. Check it when you are finished with the inspection. Is it in the same position as when you started?

- **Power Outlets**

  ✓ Are there enough power outlets?

  ✓ Are there enough outlets in places you'd like them to be?

  ✓ What is the power coming into the trailer? 30-amp, 50-amp, or more?

- **Exterior Lighting**

  ✓ Connect the trailer to the tow vehicle power (in the case of a trailer) or turn on the food truck headlights and check all of the exterior lights, running lights, headlights, accessory lights, brake lights, etc.

  ✓ Does it have LED light strips?

  ✓ Do the exterior lights attract attention to the business?

- **Water System**

  ✓ Fill the fresh water tank so you can test the gray tanks. Fill the gray tank by running the sinks. Check the status indicators (if you have them) to see if it accurately measures the level of water in the gray tank.

✓ Check the hot water heater to make sure it properly heats the water. Use a thermometer because your health department will!

✓ Follow all the plumbing, checking for leaks.

- **Kitchen Safety**

  ✓ Check to make sure it has a fire extinguisher and look at the label to make sure it hasn't expired.

  ✓ Bring a small can of gas to spray at the carbon monoxide detector (if your state requires them) to make sure it works.

  ✓ Test the hood and fans. Light a match and put it out make sure the smoke from it gets pulled out.

  ✓ Check the cleaning dates on the hood fire suppression system.

  ✓ Remove the hood filters and check for the greasy build up all the way up the stack to the roofline.

  ✓ When you get on the roof checking for water damage, pull the cap to the exhaust fans, and check the wear on the belts, the cleanliness of the cap, and the stack above the roofline.

- **Power System**

  ✓ Locate all GFCI outlets (the one with the test button in the middle). Press the test button and make sure that pops out the reset button.

  ✓ Connect to shore power and make sure it works.

  ✓ How large is the generator (assuming there's an onboard generator at all)?

  ✓ Will the generator power everything at once?

  ✓ How loud is the generator?

✓ Test each outlet and verify all the wired homerun, meaning each outlet is on its own breaker. Kitchen equipment is power-hungry, and you don't want to be tripping breakers all the time.

- **Quality Control**

✓ Check for screws all around the interior and exterior that never hit the stubs. Often the manufacturer will miss the stud and just put a glob of silicone in there.

✓ Check the trim that has been screwed but not glued, so it pokes out between the screws.

✓ Check the paneling that has waves in between the rivets.

✓ Push against the interior and exterior paneling, checking for soft spots or the paneling that is not attached.

✓ Look for rust, and dents for unnecessary holes both inside and out.

✓ Are the electric lines running inside the walls, outside the walls in conduit, or just insulated wires stapled to the walls?

✓ Are the walls free from holes? Smooth and cleanable is the standard.

- **Water Damage**

✓ Walk around the trailer and meticulously check for the slightest bubble or depression in the sides and the roof of the trailer. This is the tell-tale sign of water damage or delamination of the sides. If there are bubbles, DO NOT BUY!

✓ Get on the roof on your hands and knees to check for cracks in the sealant put around the pipes and openings. It's normal to find a small crack to be filled with a $5 sealant, but it's a sign that the trailer hasn't been cared for.

✓ Check the interior ceiling to look for any bubbles or soft spots. Especially check next to the exhaust vents, hoods, and air conditioning.

✓ Step down hard on the floor, all around the edges of the kitchen. Make sure there are no soft spots in the floor.

✓ Check under the kitchen sink and the hand wash sink to make sure water has not leaked from the pipes.

✓ Are there gutters along the sides? This is good for preventing water damage in the future.

✓ Open basement compartments and feel the bottom of each compartment to check for any wetness or soft spots where the wood has rotted out.

- **Gray Tanks**

✓ Does it have a tank flush? This is an EXTREMELY helpful feature. Not required but helpful.

✓ Are you required to have a grease trap separate from the gray tank?

- **Tires**

✓ Get down ON THE GROUND and look carefully at the tires on both sides of the tread. Is one side worn down significantly because they were not rotated? Check each tire.

✓ What brand are the tires? Are they the cheap tires, or did they get the more expensive Michelin or Goodyear tires?

✓ Check the tire pressure, especially if you plan on buying the trailer.

- **Underneath**

✓ Get on your back and crawl underneath. Look for any obvious problems or signs of damage.

✓ Is the underbelly entirely enclosed, or are the tanks on the bottom unprotected?

✓ What is the condition of the leaf springs, shocks, springs, and wheel wells?

✓ When was the last time the maintenance was performed on the axles and wheel bearings?

- **Cold Weather Service**

✓ Are the drainpipes fully enclosed?

✓ Are there electric heaters for the Water and Waste tanks?

- **Cooling**

✓ Turn on the air conditioning for 3 minutes. By this point, the air coming out should be ice cold.

✓ Is there only one air conditioning unit?

✓ Are the air conditioning units loud?

✓ Can the AC run at the same time as the hood?

✓ Check the ceiling vent fans. Are they the small kind where the blades only take up $1/3^{rd}$ of the size of the vent opening or are they the large Maxx Air fans which are far more efficient?

✓ The AC may not be of any use if you have a hood but if one exists on a used model, you expect it to work whether you use it or not.

- **Are Extras Included?**

✓ Battery or two?

✓ Spare tire? Is it a donut or a full spare?

✓ Will it come with the propane tanks?

✓ Inverter? Charger?

- **Sounds**

✓ Make sure the fans don't rattle.

✓ Listen for refrigeration & freezer compressors.

✓ Listen to the fryers when they kick on.

✓ Listen to the hood motors and AC.

- **Leveling and Stabilizing**

✓ Check the stabilizers. Are they powered or manual? If they are powered, are they so slow that it will be annoying to do each time?

- **Kitchen Equipment**

✓ Verify the wattage of the microwave. Fill a microwave-safe container with 8 oz. (1 cup) of tap water, measure its temperature, and write it down. Place the container in the microwave. Set the timer for 1:03 and hit start. (If yours is a mechanical timer-type, with just a dial, use a stopwatch; this must be accurately timed). Carefully measure the end' temperature and multiply the difference by 38.8. The result is the approximate energy gain in watts. Wondering about those 3 seconds? It takes about that long for the magnetron tubes filament to heat and start to fire and we want exactly 1 minute of heating. Compare that wattage number you computed to the wattage listed on the microwave. If the difference is over 200 watts, that microwave needs repair.

✓ Has the cutting board cover for the 3-compartment sink been lost?

✓ Will the fridge be large enough to handle your business needs?

✓ Does the fridge run on electricity only, or is propane/electric/DC?

✓ Does the flat top grill heat properly across all burners and evenly on the surface?

✓ Can you verify the recovery time of the fryer? That is the time it takes for the fryer to regain the cooking temperature once the product is dropped into the shortening.

✓ Do the fry baskets have broken or missing wires?

✓ Look inside and under all cooking equipment for grease spills or leaks. Check all the grease trays for holes, broken welds, or splits.

✓ Follow all propane lines checking for leaks, line condition, and cleanliness.

✓ Are the pots and pans clean to your standards?

✓ Look for carbon (black) build-up on griddles, fryers, pans, and steam tables

✓ Look for mineral deposits inside the steam tables.

✓ Is there enough counter space for your menu?

✓ Is the sink layout legal for your area? Size, position, drain boards, correct number.

- **Height**

✓ If you'll be storing the trailer in a garage, check the exact height of the trailer plus the air conditioning units/vents/exhaust hoods, etc. on top. Make sure you'll fit and know the clearance when driving.

✓ If you are very tall, check the ceiling height. It can be different in converted cargo trailers, so make sure you won't feel too cramped.

✓ Remember that a taller trailer feels wonderfully roomy but may require you to pull over and wait out a windstorm.

- **For Trucks Only**

✓ What is the tow rating on the hitch?

✓ Check the sticker on the windshield to see when the previous owner got their last oil change.

✓ Make sure it doesn't leak oil. This is the first sign of engine trouble.

✓ Unless you are a mechanic, bring along a professional to assess the engine and the drive train.

- **For Trailers Only**

✓ Be certain to check the exact amount your tow vehicle can tow. Oftentimes, vehicles have many options that will determine the actual rating of that vehicle. Check your VIN number and consult the actual owner's manual.

✓ If you'll be towing with anything other than a truck, make sure your vehicle has an integrated brake controller, or else you'll have to budget another $400 to buy one. A brake controller is NOT optional!

✓ Be absolutely certain there is enough clearance between the trailer and the back of your vehicle. People often add a cooler, generator, or propane cages, and that may not leave enough room. Just because you hook up and see space does not mean it's a fit. Turn a hard right and left and check to make sure the trailer won't hit the back of your truck.

✓ Remember you'll be adding inventory and water, and do not get within 80% of your max weight!

CHAPTER 4:

What Are the Best Sources of Financing

It is imperative that you have sufficient capital to not only start your business but also to maintain it. It isn't until you project your costs, will you know if you currently have enough funds out of pocket to make your business idea happen. There are several options if you do not have sufficient capital out of pocket. Obviously, the best choice would be to save until you can pay for most of your startup and operational expenses out of pocket to eliminate a lot of unnecessary debt in the beginning. But we all know, especially since the economic decline in 2007/2008 that is very difficult these days.

There are various types of financing and we will talk about the most common ones in this chapter:

Debt Financing

Debt financing is obtaining capital such as loans without giving up equity or ownership in the business to obtain it. Debt financing can come from financial institutions, lending institutions, and non-traditional lenders.

The lending requirements vary among lending institutions. They do not give you money just because you are starting a business or because you are Mr. Nice Guy or Girl.

They are a business themselves and one of the ways they can earn revenue and stay in business is a client's ability to pay back the capital they borrowed plus the agreed-upon interest.

Because lending institutions are dependent on a client's ability to pay, they implement qualification thresholds to eliminate a lot of the risks in lending. Typical lending considerations although vary between place to place, they all have typical minimums between all of them which are dependent on the capital amount you are requesting and other requirements. They will evaluate you based on the financial documents you submit as part of your loan application. The typical documents they will assess are:

- **Satisfactory FICO Score and Credit History**: Scores they typically have accepted were at minimums of 680-720 or higher. Some institutions have accepted lower credit scores of around 650 but it was more likely due to the individuals, other financial documents surpassed the institution's expectations.

- **3 Years of Most Recent Tax Returns**: This is how they evaluate your income level interests to determine that if you had to return to the workforce, would your expected salary be sufficient to pay back a loan for the capital amount you want to request.

- **Collateral**: The higher the capital amount you are requesting, the more they will expect you to have assets that are a 1-to-1 match in value. For example, if you are seeking $200K or more in the capital, they will definitely expect you to have home equity of an equal amount. The purpose is the financial institutions want their money back ASAP and if you default, they want to be able to liquidate the assets you have quickly to get it.

- **Industry Experience and Business Plan**: They typically ask for your resume to show your industry experience as well as your business plan. These two sets of documents provide them with the opportunity to see if you have experience in the industry you would like to start a business in and if you have a strong plan in place to make this business successful.

- **Can Contribute At Least 25-30% Out-of-Pocket**: This is a set in stone standard for the most financial institutions. This also helps them see that you have faith in your business idea.

- **Industry and Growth Trends**: They will look into the industry and see if it is growing, declining, or a stagnant market. Sometimes the approval process isn't about you and your talents and plans, sometimes they will not approve someone because the industry they are getting into is declining and that scares the financial institutions.

- **A Written Explanation of the Amount Seeking and a Breakdown of the Associated Costs**: Financial institutions will often request a written statement of the amount you are seeking, plus a breakdown of what you would like to use the funds for, and any associate costs. They want to see what you will do with the funds or if it was you just picking a number out of thin air.

Personal Financing

- Out-of-Pocket: Minimum of 25-30%

- Family/Friends

Equity Financing

- Trusted Business Partner with capital to contribute

- Investor

Other

Crowd funding is a viable option depending on the type of business you would like to start. Most business owners who use crowd funding to fund their businesses and are unsuccessful as it is typically because they assume that they can just design a campaign without promoting it. Like the internet, there are millions of people on crowd funding sites, so how will people find you if you do not talk about it or promote your campaign.

Scale down/start small to where it fits your financial means is the most logical step if you cannot get outside funding for your business. There is nothing wrong with starting your business on a smaller scale so you don't incur any unnecessary expenses from the start. This also is a true benefit to people with minimal industry experience as starting small is less of a risk to obtain that experience. If an aspiring entrepreneur can make their concept work on a smaller scale, then they can grow into their ideal scenario instead of starting big and failing and most of the times and not being able to adjust to the failure or adapt to it.

Free Grants: As mentioned at the beginning of this guide, although there are free grants out there on legitimate sites such as *www.grants.gov*, very rarely if at all are these grants designed for the general public. Grants are made available because an economic development agency or governmental institution, whether it is a federal, state, or a local one has tasks within the community they need to solve and will occasionally recruit businesses to help them solve those economic issues. Thus grants are offered as a way of bringing those specific businesses they need to solve those issues.

For example, a hair salon very rarely will qualify for a grant because most salons don't solve an economic need.

CHAPTER 5:

Getting Licenses and Permits for Your Food Truck

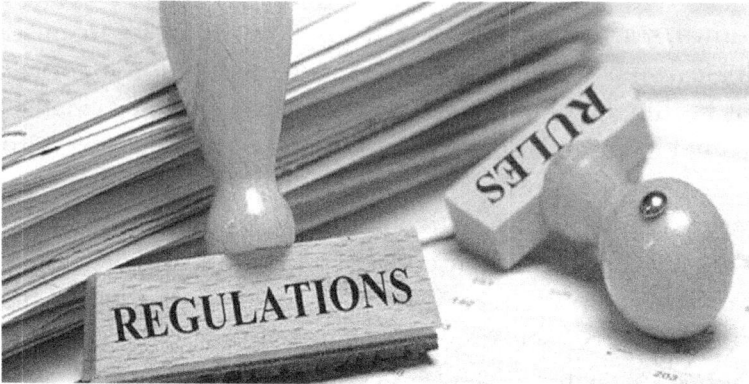

Getting the licenses and permits for your food truck is probably the most important part of the preparation process; the process of preparing to open your own food truck business. A lot of people don't consider this part of the process exciting, but it's a necessary part for people that believe in starting their business in the only way possible. One of the biggest focus on getting a permit and license is adhering to the official codes and regulations associated with starting a food truck business. Food trucks, in fact, used to have a questionable stigma, until stricter health codes and sanitary regulations were introduced across the United States.

To get started, you can always contact your state's local department of health to learn more information about handling a food-related business. On an interesting note, the types of foods you handle may change the definition of what you're supposed to represent in accordance with the current health regulations. People that sell prepackaged foods aren't considered food handlers, and typically have fewer requirements appointed to them than a person that handles food. People that deal with unwrapped food and take care of their preparation are known as food handlers, so they naturally have specific regulations they must meet before they start handling food on a daily basis, all to meet their state's health standards.

Of course, anyone who wants to run a good truck should know that they're subject to getting evaluated by a health inspector on occasions, notably when you first establish your business. To provide an example, a health inspector may request information to verify factors as seen in the following paraphrased list from another East Coast location within the United States:

- Proof of ownership, a proper license and/or identification for the vehicle

- A District Food Manager Identification Card

- Food-purchase record storage and/or record-keeping

- Proof that your commissary, service support facility, and/or depot meet the vending unit's operation needs

- A copy of your service support facility's license and/or a recently conducted inspection's report

Most food trucks and other food-related vehicles are inspected at least once every year. Many of these inspections happen on a random basis, so as a food truck vendor you should be prepared for when the occasion happens.

Health inspectors generally check your food storage methods, mainly seeing if your storage methods spoil food and if that food's being stored at the correct temperature. They also check all of the associated equipment that you may use to prepare various foods, in addition to any sinks and/or water supplies stored in the vehicle. They also check the garages and/or the commercial kitchen associated with a food truck, typically on a frequent basis. This ensures that those facilities are kept up to the current health standards, especially if associated with a food truck.

Specialized Insurance for the Food Street Vendor and Food Truck

You may consider them a moving food store, much like a café, restaurant, or a bistro, without walls and locality permanence. To the insurance companies, the food road seller that shows their delicacies on the other side or curb, or along the road just as the food truck that moves from a worksite to a business site so as to cater for the hungry patrons outside are both in their very own business class in terms of indemnity coverage.

With a certain risk exposure that separates every one of these industry businesses from the snack retail outlet or the standard food, the food road seller and food truck needs their very own particular insurance strategy, customized expressly to the different risks they face on an everyday premise. What kinds of business coverage do the mobile food shops, for example, the road seller and food truck really require? The following outlines the essential points being referred to.

Food Street Vendor

Pre-arranged to business interests, the urban communities, towns, and numerous regions that dot the national guide disperses licenses to allow the road dealers to offer prepared food and natural products to the passing pedestrians on the streets, lanes, and walkways.

Delicious tastes, presentation, and smells entice passersby with their offering of pizza, tacos, hot pretzels, French fries, hot dogs, subs, etc. The related insurance coverage incorporates the property, stock, supply, general risk, auto liability, and products liability.

The related and coverage premiums, however, are custom-made to the individual seller through any of the related nation-wide insurance agencies to improve and tweak the commercial security.

Food Serving Truck

Like the street seller, but with its own arrangement of individualized coverage needs because of its method of truck commute, the food serving truck is likewise outfitted with a city, town, or a city license to operate. Giving a full menu of cold and hot food and snacks to its ravenous clients, the food truck requires the protection coverage of the merchant and more: property, stock, supply, product liability, general liability, auto liability, just as the real truck insurance coverage. Obviously, interested individuals are best off, digging further into the related insurance matters with an expert that has their eventual benefits at the top of their priority list, and can make the person in question into an educated insurance customer.

New York Food Trucks for Happy Eating

Food trucks have become a staple of New York City. You can't walk more than two blocks without seeing somebody offering food in a little white holder. Dutch settlers introduced pushcart food in 1691 initially. The food probably won't have been as delectable in those days; however, it was a simple method to get a brisk brute during your mid-day break.

The food has changed; however, the idea remains the same. New Yorkers have occupied individuals and nobody has the time to sit down in an eatery and have lunch.

New York food trucks have and consistently will cater to the lunch crowd. Rather than making do with a chicken, rice, or a hotdog, you can appreciate gourmet dinners, everything from waffles to tacos to dumplings. It is all excellent food; thus the long queues folded over the blocks. There are a lot of incredible trucks to attempt, however, let us talk about certain trucks you can't pass up.

Everybody realizes breakfast can be eaten at any time of the day. If you understand how astonishing waffles are, look at Waffles and Dinges. Get it?

The Dinges, incorporate *dulce de leche*, Belgian chocolate fudge, pecans, bananas, whipped cream, and so forth. Furthermore, remember the scoop of vanilla frozen yogurt! What sort of waffle would it be? Other than the customary sweet waffles, there is an appetizing waffle; however, it is just for the adventurous. It has pulled BBQ pork and coleslaw slathered on top. Try it before you judge!

Prefer BBQ without the waffle? At that point head over to Korilla BBQ, a food truck serving classic Korean recipes in contemporary structures.

Choose a filling, for example, chicken thighs, rib-eye, pulled pork, or tofu, and afterward stick it in a burrito, Chosun bowl, or tacos. At that point obviously, you can add on some kimchi, cheddar, salsa hot sauce, and other ingredients.

Not in the mood for zesty kimchi? Maybe a customary Greek food truck would better fill your stomach. Souvlaki GR food truck is so staggeringly scrumptious that they presently have a café on the Lower East Side. Other than the standard pita souvlaki, you can likewise feast on a Greek burger, salad, fries, and choco-freta, a Greek chocolate wafer bar. Sometimes the basic food is simply the best!

The choices don't stop there, there is the Bistro Truck serving Mediterranean cooking, the Big D's Grub Truck dishing out the grinder and tacos sandwiches, the Rickshaw Dumpling Truck steaming dumplings, and what else?. So much more! NYC food trucks have become an incredible marvel. When your stomach is grumbling, stop by one of these astonishing trucks for some grub.

CHAPTER 6:

Strategies and Menu Ideas

Who are your customers? Identify your target customers. How to know your market? What are the best products?

Plan Your Menu

In order to plan the perfect menu, you should ask yourself some questions that will make the business of choosing which foods should go on the menu easy for you. Here are some of those questions:

1. What's easy for you to cook? Can you cook hotdogs without burning either side? Can you flip pancakes like a pro? Do you know how to make delicious patties with just the right amount of condiments? You have to determine what you can cook so you can narrow your choices down instead of overwhelming yourself with the thought that you should cook every dish in the world.

2. What's your specialty? Of course, there are a couple of dishes that you know how to cook and that's exactly why you're planning to open a food truck business. But, there will always be a dish that you're confident about and that you know you can cook better than anyone else does. What is it? Think about it and think about how you can use it for this business. For example, you can cook Fettuccine Alfredo-like you're from Italy and you know that it tastes different from what others make. Think about that and see if you can make more variations, or if you want to feature the said dish with some side dishes. This way, when people think about your food truck, they'll remember your specialty dish and they'd keep coming back for more.

3. Which ingredients are easy to get around you? Maybe, you're planning to put up a hotdog food truck but you're in an area where there are loads of fish and fresh produce around. What do you do? Will you still get meat for the hotdog from another town, or will you make use of the ingredients close to you, especially if you can actually make great dishes out of them? Sometimes, it's important to look around and see what you can do with what you have around because that will save you a lot of money, and may even make you closer to people around you, as well!

4. What do the people around you love to eat? Or, what are they looking for? Get to know your customers. Of course, it may be impossible to meet each and every one of them but it wouldn't be impossible to observe and make a general assessment as to what kind of food they enjoy the most. This way, when you set up your food truck, you can be sure that at least one or two people will try what you have to offer. On the other hand, you can also observe what's lacking in the area and you can check whether you can give them that or not. For example, New York is full of these pizza, pretzel, and hotdog kiosks, and food trucks. However, there's a lack of sushi trucks or even trucks that sell ramen or maybe even something organic. You

see, there are so many things that you can cook and offer people, so research on that. If you offer people what they're missing or what's not currently available in the area, you just might get a positive response because more often than not, people want to try what they still haven't before.

5. What kinds of food can customers easily take with them? As a customer, it's important to know that you'll be able to eat something easy to bring, especially because most people are on the go these days. So, it's essential that you make the packaging of your products efficient so that people won't have a hard time with them.

6. Which ingredients are too costly? Think about the dishes that you'll be making and see to it that you're not wasting too much money on ingredients, especially if you don't have enough budget, to begin with. Think about a dish that you can make and you know you're good at, that won't cost too much. It's important not to waste a lot of money when you're only starting.

7. Which ingredients are portable? There may be times when you lack ingredients in the truck and you have to buy some more from the nearest store, but what if it's a couple of miles away? You have to think about the ingredients that you'll be using, too, because they're important when it comes to the dishes that you'll be cooking.

8. Which food products are easy to re-heat? If you're planning to set up an Industrial Catering Vehicle, it would be important to know which food products can you easily re-heat without them losing their quality, and you have to learn which foods don't get spoiled easily, as well, as you'll be traveling around a lot.

9. Will you focus on your expertise, or are you willing to try something new? Suppose you're famous for creating delicious and appetizing cupcakes. Are you going to sell them or make

them the focus of your business? Or are you also willing to learn how to make other dishes and make use of them, too? Diversity is very important when it comes to food trucks, but being confident with what you're doing is also one of the biggest keys to success.

10. Will your menu always be your menu, or will you be able to change it? It's importance to observe whether your customers like your menu or not, and be open to changes if needed.

11. What time will you be open and on which days? You have to create a schedule and you have to stick to it because when your customers notice that you're not around for a day or two, and when they feel like you're not open at a certain given time, they may think that you're no longer in business or that you're not serious with what you're doing, and that's definitely something that you shouldn't allow to happen.

Then, when you finally decide what kind of menu you are going to offer your customers, you have to make sure that you get to cook the food properly and that you think about some guidelines that will help your customers create the perfect food truck dish. These guidelines are:

1. You have to make sure that you are consistent. Consistent in what, you ask? Well, consistent when it comes to making good food. Remember that you're not planning to have people eat at your place and never come back anymore, right? So, you have to make sure that you always get to create good food so when they recommend you to other people, they won't be embarrassed that they did so and you'd gain more customers, too.

2. Make food that you won't have a hard time serving. Food trucks are mainly created for people who are on the go so you have to learn how to work fast but still make sure that what

you're doing is right. Create dishes that are easy to serve so people won't be bored and there won't be much pressure on you.

3. And, make food that won't spoil even if it's taken on the road. You have to expect that your customers will take their orders with them on the go. Of course, some people may stay at your food truck and eat but most of the customers may choose to just take their orders with them. Take care of the packaging and make sure to use only the right kinds of ingredients.

Pricing Your Menu

Pricing your menu properly can be scary especially if you have never sold anything. Assigning a fair value to products can be difficult for some people.

Make prices too low, and you may be quite busy but have **little to show for it**.

Go too high and no one stops to eat. In pricing, you have to be Goldilocks, finding that 'just right' balance of price vs. value.

Value goes beyond high-quality products on your menu. Value is perceived in the delivery of the said menu. A clean cart or trailer, fantastic service, witty interaction with your guests, and a location convenience, **all play a part in adding value** to your products.

How many times have you groaned at the price of toilet paper at a convenience store only to buy it anyway because it saved you time? Your location provides a food choice for your guests plus saving them time, gasoline, and trouble.

I work on the beach a lot, so my base pricing is higher than other areas in the USA. I once set up 5 days a week at a very remote subdivision being built by a developer that had 100 to 150 workers. It was located an hour inland and 20 minutes from the nearest town. The closest and the only food was pizza, with limited toppings, made in an old dirty Exxon station with 2 gas pumps (the kind that dinged every gallon!).

I set up my shop in the middle of the subdivision construction and used my higher beach pricing without a problem. By the end of the construction, nearly the entire group of workers was eating with me. This was one of those situations where I actually did work about 3 hours a day from prep to service to clean up. Because the entire site shut down at once for lunch, I had to have help handling the crowd, so the workers had enough time to eat.

Pro Tip: Location Convenience Adds a Significant Value in Justifying Higher Prices

When I price my food, I include everything that a guest could possibly want on the product that I would not upcharge them for. Then I look at different price points and ask, 'Would I pay that amount, and is that price comparable to the competition?'

Pro Tip: You Don't Have To Be Cheaper To Be Perceived As Better

The hamburger example cost us $1.44 and could sell for $5.75, giving a 25.04% food cost. It was fully dressed in common condiments.

$6.00 is a quite common (which we are under) street price for a ¼ lbs. burger. What if another area would not pay that and I had to drop it to $5.00 to stay competitive? No problem, food cost is still a great 28.80%.

How about an economically depressed area and you had to match a Wendy's single pricing? The average price of a single cheese is $4.19 at Wendy's. Using that price, our food cost would be 34.37%, and that puts us in the danger zone for profitability. No need to panic or throw in the towel.

Pro Tip: Bundle High Food Cost Items with Low-Cost Sides and Drinks to Lower the Overall Food Cost, and Increase the Ticket Averages

This increases the perceived value of the purchase and leaves the guest feeling like they got a good deal. Best of all it **lowers the overall food cost** and the impact of the fixed costs on your bottom line.

Take our $1.44 cost for the burger and add in a chip and soda. Our total costs go to $2.03 and we can sell it for $6.69 like Wendy's, giving us a better food cost at 29.89%. Pricing your ala carte chips and soda at $1.25 and $1.75 respectively also gives a discount to your guests for purchasing a combo. They saved 50 cents and will feel better about the purchase.

Pro Tip: Suggestively Sell High Value/Low-Cost Add-on Items like Chili or Bacon at Every Opportunity

If you don't want to deal with a combo pricing, **knowing your food cost** for each item will signal when you should suggestively sell it and what to recommend.

When our $4.19 (34.37% FC) Burger is ordered, our response should be: 'What kind of chips and drink would you like to add?' (Notice this question requires them to answer with a flavor rather than a 'NO' had you asked, 'Would you like chips and a drink?'). Even without offering a combo deal most guests will take at least a drink and of course, this **lowers the overall food cost of that ticket**.

Pro Tip: Pricing a Menu for Profitability is Extremely Important

However, understanding your costs, how to suggest sell, up-sell, and create daily features will bring more profits in the long run.

As you are playing with the menu price for each item, start with a 25% food and paper cost. It is OK to be above your goal percentage with some products. Those are the ones you train yourself to suggestive sell high-profit side items to complete the meal and up your check average.

Pro Tip: Have Different Menus (and Price Structures) For Different Vending Sites and Events

Create different price structures for different events. The entry fees vary so much from event to event that you may as well be prepared now with different pricing structures.

Now you have an idea of how to portion and price your food for profitability. Let's discuss how to price your food for the ease of operations. You may have noticed that most vendors will price on an even dollar value and include the sales tax. Personally, I'm not afraid of making changes, but for speed, I only price on the quarter and I do include the sales tax.

This makes determining net sales (and food cost) slightly harder, as one mathematical step has to be added. For the ease of explanation in all examples, I assume tax to be added on after rather than included in the menu pricing.

Round off the prices on your menu as you need to do the math comfortably. Include the tax rate at the listed price. That means a menu price of $7.00 is really $6.60 for you and $0.40 for the taxman. (Based on a 6% sales tax, your tax rate could be different).

Pro Tip: To finalize the pricing, look at your competition

What are they selling and how is it priced? Most vendors, at the very least, use Facebook and post a picture of their menu. See if your pricing is in line with your direct competitors.

Going cheaper does not guarantee success, sometimes it comes off as just that CHEAP. That being said you can be successful with a discounted price compared to the competition if you **market the price paired with quality and taste**.

Remember when Pepsi first started? (I don't either, look it up!) They sold their product for the same price as Coca-Cola but **doubled the amount of soda** in a container. Today Pepsi and Coke sell for the exact same amount, except for coupons and discounts, of course.

If you want to be cheaper than the competition, you will need to **stress your quality and service** to be superior to the more expensive vendors. Then execute your plan.

Pro Tip: Price Your Menu Similar to Your Competition

DO NOT BE AFRAID to price higher.

The point of difference in your foodservice business must be in the overall Guest Experience you provide. What is that you ask???

There are 4 elements that define a food service operation no matter what the size, service style, or sales volume is. I refer to those elements as QSC^2:

Quality: Pertains to high standards (freshness, taste, temperature, smell, etc.) yet profitable ingredients. Finished products are presented with care and respect. Attention to food detail, such as neat assembly, uniformity of hand-cut items; today's portion is exactly the same as last weeks and next weeks, etc. Quality, pertaining to food, means buying the best, fresh wholesome ingredients you can profitably afford and then preparing them in a food-safe manner that respects the ingredient. Finally, assembling and presenting a delicious, tasty, and neatly assembled product to the guest. In other words: keep hot food hot, cold food cold, and chips crispy.

Service: Fast and friendly, courteous, respectful, and inviting attitude. More attention should be given to the details, verifying the served food meets the quality standards and is going to the right person. Smiles, speed, and personality win every time.

Cleanliness: Of course, it is the sparkling, sanitary condition in your cart, trailer, or truck. Cleanliness also applies to the area surrounding your setup, your organizational skills in the kitchen, and neat and tidy areas guests may use like condiment tables.

Community: It means being a part of your community, a good neighbor if you will. It is the emotional connection your guests have towards your business: location convenience, the involvement in the local community, fundraising, going the extra mile for a special request, and providing more than that is required at catered events. Restaurant commercials you see on TV that DON'T mention food usually is tugging at your heart, creating an emotional connection to the brand.

Before you move on you should have your menu worked out, where you will get every item (with backup sources), and what equipment you will need to cool, freeze, cook, hold, and serve every product. Most importantly you should know exactly how much each product costs you and what you will sell it for.

Extras

As time goes by, you can also add more dishes on your menu and you may also add some other items in your truck that you could sell. These items include official merchandise with the name of your business, some souvenirs that customers can give away, and other things that will remind them of your business so that they won't forget it right away. Make sure though that you leave them a good impression so they'd want to buy these extra items. If you know how to plan your food truck menu, things will definitely be much easier for you!

CHAPTER 7:

The Most Integral Factors of Starting a Food Truck Business

Is The Market Saturated?

It's easy to think of the food truck industry as a new industry with relatively fewer competitors but you still need to act fast and start before your local market gets saturated. Los Angeles and New York have practically reached the saturation point. Smaller markets have fewer trucks but that is quickly changing.

The mobile food business is constantly experiencing growth and here are a few basic concepts you can follow to make good money in this industry. First of all, you should offer unique dishes not found anywhere else. As mentioned before, these could be unique variations of classic dishes. There's no need to reinvent the wheel here! One strategy you could use is to offer lower prices than your competition. But many trucks are still very successful offering premium pricing on their menu items. Finding the best locations has an impact on how many customers you'll serve in a day. But as more and more trucks are hitting the streets, you'll have a harder and harder time finding good prime locations. And this goes almost without saying that you need to serve high-quality food quickly!

As an entrepreneur, you need to be extremely organized and have the ability to make quick decisions. One example of quick decision-making is the ability to relocate if your current location isn't generating the type of income you're expecting. You will need alternate locations planned or be able to quickly get permits for other locations. Keep in mind that this is no ordinary job! Running a food truck means you'll most likely be in several locations each week and run into unforeseen challenges at every location. This can take a huge toll on a person's stamina! While owning a food truck may seem easy to do on the surface... In reality, running a food truck is probably going to be one of the most challenging jobs you will ever have!

Testing The Market

In business, you must always test the market to see what will work. After you have done your market research and have decided on the elements of your food truck, you now have to decide what you are going to serve and how much you are going to charge clients (based on the complete market analysis that you have done for your business plan).

When you have already decided on what you will offer, dive into the details. Let's start with the menu that you want to present. You must finalize the food that you are going to put on the menu. A very common mistake made by food trucks is to have a menu that is more extensive than it needs to be, or that offers too diverse a selection. A large menu overwhelms guests, slows down ordering and processing times, and takes critical space in your truck for storage that could be used for your best sellers.

It is good to have professionally designed menu boards that fit your brand, and if your truck is wrapped or decorated to draw attention from diners, your menu should look and feel consistent with that work. If your budget does not allow this kind of branding on the truck itself, chalkboard with very legible offerings works fine. At the beginning, this will give you the flexibility to alter your offerings based on actual sales before a more permanent decision can be made.

Testing the market is a very important step in opening up your food truck business because you want to know what is likely to work before you go in and invest your time, money and effort. There are several ways to test the market for your food and these include:

Research on the Success of Food Trucks like Yours

The very first thing that you should do would be to research on food similar to the one you're making. If you see that their food is popular, you can bet that your food will also be popular as well if you make it taste great. The only challenge here would be how to market your brand and how to establish a name that distinguishes you sufficiently to avoid market confusion. This should likely have been done before reaching the test market phase.

Try a Formal or Informal Survey

Another method of testing the market would be to create surveys. We love the taste-plate approach, where you invite friends and relatives to a party or gathering and offer your proposed menu for their feedback. These must be guests that you trust to give you candid feedback. You need to know if your items are too salty, or not spicy enough. This informal survey is very valuable to finalizing your menu. The exercise of making this food also gives you a feel for labor and prep time, which will help you decide if it makes sense to offer a particular item at a certain price. With the internet, this is now extremely easy to do formal surveys, because you can make use of survey apps or programs like Survey Monkey or even Google Forms. You have to just decide on the number of respondents that you would like to have for your survey and their demographic (your target market). From there, you can send out your survey and adjust your decisions on the results. If the results show that people like your idea, you may not need to make changes.

"Dry" Runs

Before you spend a ton of money on a food truck, you should rent the truck you are proposing to buy, whether it is new or used; ask for a tester that will allow you to serve your food in real-time. A poorly located fryer or a fridge that is too small will be very hard to adjust once you have paid the asking price. You may want a different truck. Similarly, if the plan is to staff the truck with one or more additional employees, you need to get in the truck with them and see how you move together, to make decisions about who will perform what functions when the truck is in operations. Finally, this gives you a chance at a festival, event, or with a prospective lunch crowd to see if your food sells, and at what price. It would never make sense to attack this business and spend the capital required for success without having tried these things.

Creating the Brand

For your brand to be effective, it must accomplish all of the following:

- It make must your business easily recognizable. The easier your business is to recognize, the more people you will attract to your business with a certain product or service. This in turn translates into more sales.

- It must be pleasing, fun, and a positive reflection on your offering. If you are all organic or locally sourced, your brand should reflect what makes you better.

The brand should be professional, and consistent with your product. Some brands do well with characters, or funny animation, a gourmet brand offering more expensive or exclusive fair, should be more serious. This is critical to avoiding customer confusion

Your brand should be highly visible, from the truck or otherwise, and unique to you, so that customers can see it and instantly recognize what you offer. Your brand is much more than a logo, or wrap on the truck, it is a feeling you are trying to share with the customer that draws them to your business. A logo is important, but all of your branded items, should be consistent with each other, and contribute to a greater understanding of your business and offerings.

All of the best brands are easy to remember and simple in design. The very best brands are the ones that you don't need to explain. Once a person sees the brand, he or she will immediately know what your food truck is all about.

The best brands also hold an emotional appeal to the target market. The emotional connection that you will make will depend on the demographic and psychographic profile of the target market. In other words, you have to know what makes them "tick". You have to know what strikes their emotional strings and work your brand identity on that.

Lastly, your brand identity should be consistent. If you have multiple trucks, they should be similarly decked out with signage or wraps.

Food trucks are no different than brick and mortar restaurant establishments; both must rely on steady customer traffic to generate cash flow. The reason why we treat customers like a 'football super-star' is that it costs eight times (8X) more to acquire a new customer in comparison to getting repeat business.

Building a loyal following in your customer base is more cost-effective, so why not remember your loyal customers by personally recognizing them each time they frequent your establishment.

If you do this, your brand loyalty will be reinforced by the loyal customer bringing friends to enjoy the same 'football super-star' status they have come to expect.

Logo Design (Brand Recognition): A company's logo is equally as important as your business name and the type of service provided. The logo establishes your brand and differentiates your business from competitors. If executed correctly, your company's brand will be recognized by consumers as an establishment that delivers a consistent, quality product and an exceptional service at a price that meets a consumer's budget.

Do an internal assessment of successful company brands that deliver on the following: consistency, quality, service, and price. In the U.S. three companies come to mind that delivers on these attributes.

- Starbucks™ meets the demands of many coffee drinkers; and

- Chick-fil-A® and Culver's® meets the demands of many fast-casual consumer tastes.

If you have patronized any of the previously mentioned establishments throughout the United States, you will find that each company flawlessly executes consistency, quality, service, and price.

Granted, this is attributed to their training program for employees, but their reputation of meeting expectations is what consumers have come to know based on the experience they have encountered when frequenting these establishments.

Brand recognition is important and must be thought out in the planning aspect of kicking off your food truck concept.

Testimonial: Now you are probably thinking this is going to cost me a lot of money to pull off? It is not that expensive. Here is how my logo design started.

I am no artist, but I had a visual concept of what I wanted my company logo to look like. First, I scribbled a pencil design of what I wanted on paper (see the front cover); Second, I asked a young man from my church that was going to school for graphic design to fine-tune what I developed on paper into something more appealing. He did a free-hand revision of my design on paper and presented multiple different versions and concepts for me to consider.

I ended up selecting three out of five of the designs he drew by free-hand and provided these sketches to a company called 'Logo Mojo' to transform the concepts into a professional look. Logo Mojo (now Deluxe) offers affordable logo packages for customers to select from. My logo was processed in less than 45 days, in fact, I was so pleased with their quality of work that I ended up purchasing two logo designs.

Words of Wisdom: Remember, every aspect of your business is important especially as a small business owner. Your business logo design need not be an aspect you put substandard effort into. If your company logo looks amateurish or unattractive, prospective patrons may associate those aspects with your business. Don't be cheap, hire this portion of your business development out to an expert.

Legal Business Structure: The legal registry and setup of your business entity will vary by state. The primary benefits of registering your business include the protection of your personal assets from your business assets to include certain tax advantages. The five legal business structures in the U.S. are:

- Sole Proprietorships

- Partnerships

- Corporations

- Limited Liability Company (LLC)

A **sole proprietorship** is a business owner of an unincorporated business by himself or herself. Individuals operating their business in this form will use their Social Security Number (SSN) to legally identify the business. Income generated or losses incurred in relation to the operation of the business are reported on the business owner's individual tax return.

A **partnership** is a single business where two or more business owners share ownership of the business. As a contributing owner of the business, each business partner shares in the profits, losses, or investment of that business. The business is registered with the IRS and the partners are required to file an annual return of income on the IRS Form 1065, U.S. Return of Partnership Income.

Business entities formed as a **corporation** are the most complex of the five business legal structures and generally have costly administrative fees and complex tax and legal requirements. A business formed under this structure is an independent legal entity owned by shareholders; any actions and debts incurred by the business is the responsibility of the corporation.

A **Limited Liability Company (LLC)** is a business structure allowed by a statute enacted by a particular state. There are some restrictions on the type of business that may be formed under such a business entity; however, food trucks are not restricted from being formed as an LLC. An LLC provides the limited liability benefits of a corporation to protect your business and has tax advantages of a partnership to report profits and losses on a business member's personal tax return.

The IRS and Small Business Administration (SBA) are excellent resources to determine which business entity to form your company. The SBA website goes into great detail in assessing the pros and cons of each of the five aforementioned business structures. A Certified Public Accountant (CPA) or a tax consultant is also a good resource to seek advice for your situation.

If you are not proficient in preparing your business taxes, you will need to rely on the expertise of a tax consultant or CPA while operating your company for the preparation and filing of sales tax remittances to the state, payroll for employees, and the federal and state income tax filings at the end of the year.

Words of Wisdom: Remember to protect your assets by legally registering your company in a manner that protects your personal assets from your business assets. Read the statutes for your state on establishing an LLC, Partnership, and S-Corp. It is not as hard as you think. Take your time, read, and research.

Registering Your Business Federal/State/City: I always caution any future business owners for using his Social Security Number (SSN) to identify their business as a sole proprietor would be required to do. You make your own determination, but on the day of privacy violation, personal data breaches by computer hackers, and identity theft, pursue the other four options of registering your business with the IRS instead.

The guide in the succeeding section should be used as a general outline of the steps to take in the registration of your business in the state you plan to do operations.

Business requirements to set up any business starts with the Federal/IRS and the Secretary of State for the state you reside in. Most Secretary of State websites have a '*Doing Business within [state name]*' checklist for new businesses.

County and city ordinance requirements may also apply depending on how your business is setup. One key caveat to remember is that, not every facet of the requirements in this section covers every state; however, the process is similar in scope and you will have enough information to know where to go to obtain the required forms. Follow these steps:

1.   Federal/IRS

- Apply for a federal Employer Identification Number (EIN) from the IRS. This process may be completed online by going to *https://www.irs.gov*. Select **Apply** for an EIN and follow the steps prompted online. Most new businesses will be permitted to apply for an EIN via this method.

- Remember to print out the notice generated by your Form SS-4 online application through the IRS website and keep it for your record.

- The EIN is your business's equivalent of your personal SSN. You will use this number for all business transactions when applying for loans, credit cards, state licensing, etc.

- Place the notice you receive for your EIN in your 3-ring binder.

Review the following on the IRS website:

  o Small Business Tax Guide

  o Starting a Business and Keeping Records

  o Business Use of Your Home

2.   Registering a new LLC with [state name] Secretary of State

- Read the state statute on the LLCs and verify that the name you have selected for your business is available in the state you intend to register your LLC.

- Some states have a two-page form for a new business to fill out to register their business, which encompasses articles of organization, the designated registered agent that manages the legal aspects of the business, and managers of the LLC.

- LLCs will be required to file a bi-annual or annual report (depending on the state of the registry) stating the business is still active. There is normally a fee involved with this process.

- Check with the state you intend to register your company; the process is very similar and easy to accomplish yourself.

- Place the LLC documentation received from [state name] in your 3-ring binder.

3.   [state name] Tax Registration

- As a retail foodservice business, you will be required to pay sales taxes on the product you sell to consumers. Hence, you will need to obtain a Sales Tax Permit from the state you will conduct food truck sales; some states also call this a Sales and Use Tax.

- Go to the [state name] Department of Revenue website and obtain the required application form to register your business. Many states enable businesses to accomplish this process online.

- You will be required to provide the Legal Name of your business, and EIN or SSN if you chose to operate as a sole proprietorship.

- Many states do permit Sales Tax Permit issuances for businesses that participate in seasonal or temporary events. If your truck will be mobile and travels to different states to participate in the state fairs, festivals, gun shows, etc., you may want to consider obtaining a sales tax permit to operate in the neighboring states.

- Keep good records because you will be required to submit the sales tax remittances for all sales made to consumers, regardless if you choose to add sales tax in your transactions or include the tax into the price of the product offered for sale. Some states will also allow the retailer to retain a fee for collecting the local sales taxes (the equivalent of a rebate); check with the state's Department of Revenue, where you will operate.

- Place a copy of the Sales Permit in your 3-ring binder, and the original on your Food Service vehicle.

4.   If you will be an employer:

- If your business will have employees, you are required to apply for an income tax withholding certificate prior to withholding income taxes. Check with the [state name] Department of Labor for these requirements.

- This is considered out of scope for many new business owners electing to be an employer. Consult with a CPA or a Tax Consultant to ensure you are following the legal requirements for the state you intend to operate in and hire this task out.

5.   Food Permit or Food Service Health Permit

- The process of obtaining a food permit for food trucks is not the same for every state. It is the most challenging process of any aspect of establishing a food truck business. This is attributed to the rapid movement of the food truck industry as a whole. City, county, and state health organizations are struggling to keep up in determining the appropriate way to inspect and certify food truck operations. Not every aspect of this section may apply to your state, but if you plan on operating in neighboring states these guidelines will be handy.

- Of note, the U.S. Food and Drug Administration (FDA) issues inspection guidance at the Federal-Level. States adopt the FDA guidelines into their state Food Service Sanitation Codes at the State-Level, and Counties adopt the state guidelines at the County-Level, and Cities adopt state and county guidelines at the City-Level. Enforcement of such guidelines depends on the size of the city that resides within a county.

- **State-Level:** Check with the [state name] Department of Agriculture, [state name] Department of Public Health, or [state name] Department of Inspections and Appeals, depending on how it is organized for the state you will operate in, for the current Food Service Sanitation Code.

- **State/County-Level:** Check the [state name] website for procedures on inspecting the food service units and review this information in detail.

Review the following on the County Public Health website (as applicable for your situation):

- County and City Food Ordinances

- Submission of a Food Plan Review to operate and serve food to the public (*not applicable for every city)

- Submission of a Health Permit Application

6.   Registering Your Food Truck to Operate in the City

- Not all the city and county requirements to operate your food truck or food trailer are the same for every state. Do not expect the city you will be operating in has everything outlined clearly for your business to conduct food sales. Check with your soon-to-be peer food truck operators and the County Clerk or City Clerk to determine what you will need. The list below is a good assessment of what you can expect.

  Review and complete the following for your County or City (as applicable for your situation):

  o **Registering Your Business Name:** Maybe applicable at the County-Level for sole proprietorships if you are registered as a business entity; if it is other than a sole proprietor, it may be exempted.

- o **Food and Beverage Tax Registration:** Some cities add an additional tax to the state and local tax requirements for food purchases; you may be required to file a separate form for the city tax remittance in addition to the State requirement.

- o **Peddlers Permit:** This is equivalent to a traveling salesman permit; some cities require this for food trucks that are mobile.

- o **Building Permit:** Some cities require a building permit for food trucks to operate on a retail site (privately owned or public) and have the City Building Inspector verify the mobile unit is safe to operate.

- Place a copy of all the applicable aforementioned permits in your 3-ring binder, and the original on your Food Service vehicle.

Insurance: Always protect your business assets with insurance. When shopping for an insurance policy for your foodservice, seek out a single policy capable of covering your food truck or trailer, workers' compensation, and general liability.

Insurance companies are slowly gravitating to meet the needs of the food truck business owners, but unfortunately, only a handful of companies readily offer such services.

When shopping for insurance for your foodservice you will want to ensure you have the following basic coverage and benefits:

- General Liability Coverage up to $2,000,000; coverage must be aggregate

- Personal and Advertising Coverage

- Damage to premises rented to you

- Business Personal Property

- Workers Compensation (if you have employees)

- Unlimited Additional Insured

- Access to your account for the issuance of Additional Insured Forms

Many foodservice insurance companies offer a trailer endorsement for food trailers left on the premises of a location you are operating from for an event or storage at your commercial kitchen/commissary. Your personal automobile insurance policy may also provide coverage of your food trailer while towing it with your personal vehicle; check with your insurance agent.

Food Service/Local Competition: Check the local competition to assess what specific food needs are not already being met. Depending on how mature your market area is, you will find many food trucks and food trailers already serving the local community.

A word of caution though does not harass local food truck operators by asking them questions about the food truck business during their peak hours of operations, which is generally one-hour before lunch, and during the lunch hours. Remember they are running a business and expending every ounce of energy to meet the needs of their customers in providing a quality product. The best hours to check with them are one-hour after lunch, say 2 pm or in the evening.

Food truck vendors have a wealth of information that can be quite useful to you, so be courteous and respectful. They will soon be your peer in providing you future gigs they are unable to partake in because their schedule may be fully booked.

I often get invited to participate in events and festivals that I am unable to work due to other commitments, as such I share the wealth with my fellow food truck peers and they reciprocate in kind.

Finally, do not duplicate the needs of what others are already doing. Meaning, if you believe you have the best hamburgers in the world and think you can compete with McDonald's® or BURGER KING®, then ask yourself why should someone pay $7.00 for your burger when they can get a decent substitute from a restaurant chain for 1/5th of the price you charge?

The bottom line, provide a food product that is too time-consuming to duplicate at home at a cost affordable to consumers along with a taste that is unforgettably delicious.

Research Food Vending In Your Area

Start locally because your town may have restrictions on street vending. You need to know those restrictions before buying your cart, trailer, or truck.

Some cities allow vending but limit the number of permits issued or they limit the hours you are allowed to be opened.

It is possible you will have a fight on your hands if the local commissions have been influenced by brick and mortar restaurant owners. Chains don't really care but small restaurant owners do. They are afraid of competition. You can win the fight, but it may take time and possibly money.

Pro Tip: If You Are Already Struggling Financially, Find another More Accommodating Town to Start Your Food Vending Career

The next township may be a better choice anyway. It could be as simple as vending just outside the city limits on county land. The goal is to be legal while being profitable. Along this line of thinking make sure you know in what jurisdiction you plan to sell your food so you can get the correct information and fee schedules.

You will need some time to sift through all the information. The local government and health department will be the most confusing.

The good news is you can set up an appointment to meet in person and discuss any questions you may have. Get information from the horse's mouth so to speak. Just get any rules and regulations in writing or the official website link, so there will be no confusion later.

I suggest you download your state (or county/city) food codes and read them. Yes, it most likely will be confusing, however, when you start selling food you will be responsible to know the rules and a good inspector may quiz you on specific rules!

Google *'Start a mobile food business'* and add your *'city.'* Again, ignore ads and look for the state health department sites. Learn the differences between a hot dog vendor and a mobile food vendor, if your state licenses them differently. States have a variety of different names for mobile vendors and often have a different license structure for hot dog only vendors, preplaced food vendors, and non-hazardous food vendors (Kettle corn for example). These 'other' food type licenses have restrictions that don't apply to a full-fledged food trailer or truck. Other states have levels of licenses that restrict food types in different ways.

Pro Tip: Focus Only on Your State's Information from Official Government Sites

Given below is a screenshot of my results. As you will notice a generic business info site comes up before the official government information that we need.

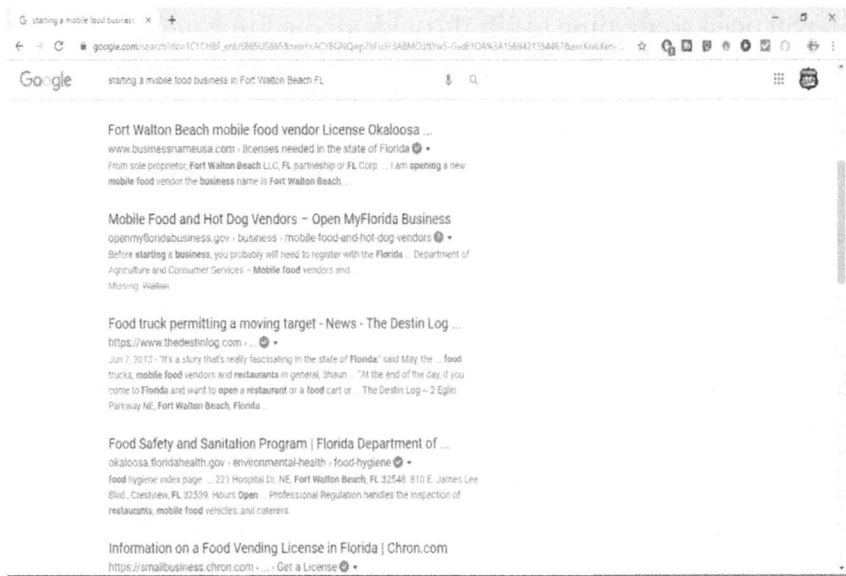

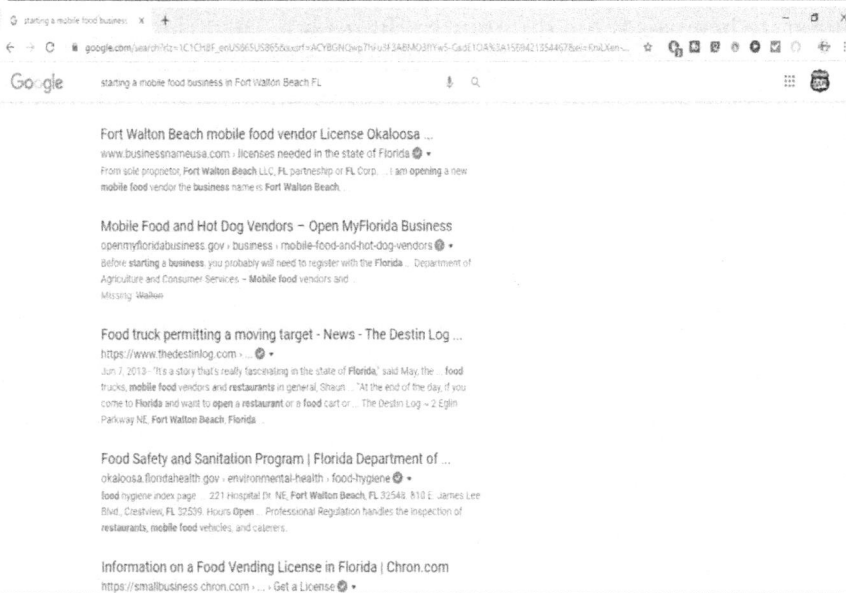

Fort Walton Beach's local government did not come up in my search on the first page. If this happens to you, go to your official city government site and search street vending rules there.

Fort Walton Beach has, as of 9/23/2019, two rules that impact street vending. One is vendors are limited to a certain area of the town if they want to vend full time. The other rule limits the number of days per month vending can take place outside of that one certain area. The only way to know that is to search the **municipal code** for Fort Walton Beach. You may have to do the same for your city.

Finish your research at the county level and then move on to the state level. Each level of government adds rules and of course more fees, permits, and licenses.

There are **no laws at the federal level** you will need to research. The US government has recommendations such as the FDA Code that the individual states base their own laws upon. As far as the health department rules, just stop at the state level.

So far, all you have researched is pertaining to food and vending (peddler) laws. There is one other MUST area to research and that is fire safety. Each local fire department will have more regulations you will be required to understand and follow. This link has the basic you will need to consider and will get you a jumping-off point for your questions and research. *https://www.nfpa.org/Codes-and-Standards/Resources/Standards-in-action/Food-truck-safety*

Why Is My State Different Than That State?

The US FDA Food code is the official set of regulations the states base their own rules on. Each state will **add, change, or delete** parts of the code to ensure the rules are consistent with other laws on the state books.

The US FDA updates these rules every 4 years (the next is in 2021) as we know the wheels of the government move slowly. Each state adopts a version and may or may not update as often as the federal level code. This creates a mass confusion regarding what is 'legal' and what is not.

There is a state using the code from 1995! (South Dakota). There is another state where the countries can choose which code year to adopt resulting in a mishmash of different code years in the same state. Crossing county lines could easily put your vehicle out of compliance.

If you are planning your business to operate from a single city or county all you need to know is one code. If your dream includes traveling a circuit in different counties or states, you will need to know those laws as well. State laws vary enough that you may not be able to take a hot dog cart (or even a trailer) on a state to state road trip.

For example, in Georgia, a hot dog cart must have 4 sinks whereas in Florida a hot dog vendor license allows only 1 sink. Both states require the license number to be prominently displayed on the cart. Each regulation can be met by a vendor with the same cart if you understand the codes and come up with acceptable solutions for both states. Think long-term about where you want to vend and how you plan on growing.

Pro Tip: Temporary Event Permits Are Generally Easier to Get If You Plan on Traveling with Your Vending Operation

Temporary permits generally have a lower threshold of requirements (often scarily lower standards) for traveling vendors or even occasional vendors. Big events may even be one-stop shops for tax collection, health permits, and fire permits for transient operators.

By this point, you have a few hours invested in research and should have a general idea about the regulatory costs before making the big purchases of a vehicle and supplies. You must understand fully your area's regulations to be able to operate within those regulations.

CHAPTER 8:

Planning For The Food Truck Business Operations

Assets				Liabilities and Equity		
Current Assets:				Current Liabilities:		
Cash		$0		Accounts Payable	$)	
Accounts Receivable	$0			Sales Taxes Payable	$)	
Less: Reserve for Bad Debts	$0	$0		Payroll Taxes Payable	$)	
Merchandise Inventory		$0		Accrued Wages Payable	$)	
Prepaid Expenses		$0		Unearned Revenues	$)	
Notes Receivable		$0		Short-Term Notes Payable	$)	
Total Current Assets			$0	Short-Term Bank Loan Payable	$)	
				Total Current Liabilities		$)
Fixed Assets:						
Vehicles	$0			Long-Term Liabilities:		
Less: Accumulated Depreciation	$0	$0		Long-Term Notes Payable	$)	
				Mortgage Payable	$)	
Equipment	$0			Total Long-Term Liabilities		$)
Less: Accumulated Depreciation	$0	$0	$0			
				Total Liabilities		$)
Total Fixed Assets			$0			
Other Assets:				Equity:		
Goodwill		$0		Owner's Equity	$)	
Total Other Assets			$0	Net Profit	$)	
				Total Equity		$)
Total Assets			$0			
				Total Liabilities and Equity		$)

Off Truck Kitchens And Commissaries

One of the most common reasons for hiring or renting a commissary is the storage of food and equipment. Today, commissaries are modeled after supermarkets, so that the customers have an easier time accessing the food, and refrigerators, ovens, etc. These benefits are nice, but costs are a material concern with commissaries. If you are running multiple trucks, it will be difficult to handle food prep and storage out of a private kitchen. Some food truckers build a second kitchen in their garages and do it that way. The space is deductible as a business expense and allows for the separation of personal food and equipment from commercial items.

Inventory And Maintenance

Food trucks need to keep an inventory of food, plates, spices, bags and any other items that may wear out or be delivered to customers during the day. If you are using a fryer, that oil can be cleaned but will have to be replaced with some frequency.

The best inventory systems monitor sales and adjust your food and equipment stores accordingly. They cost more, but the automation can save significant labor in doing food and equipment counts after every shift. These systems will also alert you on food waste, and/or deviation in portion amounts where there is a mismatch. This is important in keeping food costs manageable. If you have sufficient storage, buying in bulk will give you a lower food cost, and reduce the time, effort, and cost of multiple trips to reload. As for maintenance, you must make sure that you regularly maintain your truck, and the kitchen equipment/generators to keep things running properly. It pays to add a maintenance expense to your fixed costs so that your truck will last longer and can serve more. It is advisable to make a regular schedule for maintenance so that you can monitor the cost of your truck maintenance.

Managing Operations

Food Preparation and Procedure

Training employees to be able to prepare quality products consistently every time is critical to your business. We recommend that employees cook with full supervision for at least a week before being "certified" to prepare those items on their own.

Labor and Personnel

For a food truck business, you don't need many employees, especially if you are starting small. Typically, a food truck business will consist of a driver, two assistants in the truck (these assistants can cook, prepare food, tend the cashier, and do inventory). You can reduce these costs by handling prep yourself or including yourself as one of the staff during operations. When done properly, the food truck business requires the owner to be very hands-on to make sure everything is done properly.

Planning for Long Term Growth

After you've been in business for some time and have gotten a solid client base, you might think it is now time to grow the business. You and your partners should discuss the expected growth of the brand, and the form it will take at the time of the startup.

Does growth mean more trucks? Are you trying to open a brick and mortar restaurant? What are the goals for the timing of debt payoff to ensure that the business has the protection it needs, while still responsibly paying investors? Is a franchise system an option?

There are numerous ways to profit from your successful brand, but none of them should be seriously considered until you have been in operation for at least a year unless immediate demand will exceed expenses dramatically. There are a couple of reasons for this. As the owner, you need to know if the success of the truck is based on seasonal traffic, or circumstances, such that you have very busy months and very slow ones. Second, you need to give the business a chance to mature with all of the mistakes, issues, and problems that might have been unforeseeable at the beginning, so that you can plan for those issues at the time of expansion. Finally, premature expansion can create a capital shortage that threatens an otherwise healthy business. Be smart here.

Document Management

As your business grows, the need to keep and maintain your documents will grow with it. We highly recommend having a fireproof lockbox for key documents that do not have to be displayed on the truck itself.

You should take digital photos of all licenses and permits in case one is damaged, so you have proof of compliance while you get your replacement.

Supplies

Planning supplies is also going to be part of your operations cost, and you do not want to be in the field only to discover that you do not have everything you need to run your business.

A shortlist of things to check for would include:

- All cooking and prep tools
- Pots, Pans, Cutting/Prep boards
- Napkins
- To-go containers and customer plates
- Bags
- Straws
- Cups and lids of soda fountain used
- Dish soap
- Paper towels
- Gloves
- Trash bags
- Floor mats
- Glass and stainless steel cleaner
- Degreaser

Safety

Protect yourself

Operating a food truck does have risks. As a new business owner, you need to be prepared to protect yourself.

Deterrence of an adversary is an effective methodology regularly employed by the U.S. Military. It is demonstrated by visibly displaying strength without firing a shot. When an Aircraft Carrier Battle Group pulls into a foreign port each Warship is arrayed with visible firepower and capable men and women that know how to use that Warship. This visible deterrent makes the enemy reconsider attacking a U.S. vessel.

How does deterrence apply to you as a food truck operator? Your deterrent is the way you conduct your business operations. Make the following, part of your routine and do not make yourself an easy target:

- Be aware of your surroundings at all times.

- Do not share any info about how good or bad your sales were for the day.

- Do not share info about how much money you are making in the food truck business.

- Do not visibly display your money bag when walking to your food unit before opening or walking away from your food unit when closing.

- Be careful when going home and watch for people following you.

- Closing up shop: never leave money in the drawer overnight.

Finally, investing in a class for conceal carry is a wise business decision to consider. The class will educate you on the local laws for handguns; sharpen your skills in the use of a firearm, as this will enable you to obtain a concealed carry permit. If you live in a state or city that permits open carry, buy a gun holster and place your firearm in the holster at the end of your shift before closing if your food truck resides at a retail pad. The best defense to detract a would-be robber is to have a good offence.

Emergency Plan

Always have an emergency plan in case the weather gets bad. If you are participating in a festival event, check with the Event Coordinator and ask where the safe shelter in case of bad weather is (E.g. tornado, severe thunderstorms).

Be prepared to close down food truck operations quickly by shutting off power to your mobile food unit, secure hot cooking oil in a fryer, and use portable 6-day coolers to quickly store refrigerated foods.

Hazardous weather events are unpredictable and may shut down a festival event for an extended period and prevent operators from returning to their mobile food units until the next day. Plan for the worst and so you can reinitiate operations faster than your competitors.

Finally, maintain an Emergency Kit on your food truck equipped with a flashlight, matches, first-aid kit, a knife, and scissors.

CHAPTER 9:

Build Your Team

Hiring

When it is time to start hiring employees, write down what you want in your team. What are the essential qualities? What is the deal-breaking quality? Then stick to these. Always check references! It does help to get referrals from people you know, but it is not recommended to hire your friends and family if you can help it. Owning a business will change the way you see people. Entrepreneurs are driven and hard-working. You will quickly find out that most people are not like you. As disheartening as it is, you have to weed out the lazy, negative, and backstabbing people.

When gathering applications and resumes, screen them for spelling and grammar mistakes. Notice what the applicant looks like when they bring it in. Are they dressed well? Do they smell bad? Did they smile? These questions may seem ridiculous, but if they do not put any effort in when trying to get the job, imagine how lazy they will be when it comes to actual work. It is recommended to have another trusted person to interview with you. Another set of eyes and ears can only help you through the hiring process. If the job you are hiring for is easy to learn, hire for professionalism and attitude. Finding someone that looks you in the eye, speaks well, and is a happy person who will be much easier to work with than someone with experience but answers their phone during the interview. Imagine your customers interacting with this person.

If it feels like you are not finding the person you are looking for, keep looking! It might take time, but you do not want to make a bad hire in the beginning. This is the make or break time, and you need people you can trust.

Firing

Unfortunately, as much work as you put into hiring the right people, you will still find that people are not who you thought they were. It is important to try to train and document any counseling or talks that you have. This is so important, and even if you feel the employee is your friend, you need to document every disciplinary or corrective discussion. Keep an employee file and be honest with your employee. If you feel that their behavior is endangering their employment, let them know. Begin a performance improvement program where you meet weekly for 4-6 weeks to see if the behavior is improving. Let them know that if it isn't, they will be terminated. Usually, the behavior will quickly improve, or they will resign on their own. If not, you have ample documentation to show you were in the right to terminate.

When terminating employment, it is always a good idea to have a witness present. This protects both you and the employee. Disgruntled employees are known to make false claims, get angry, etc. A witness provides a layer of protection against lawsuits and any investigations that you may encounter regarding the firing.

Human Resources

There are many, many regulations that you must be prepared to follow when hiring employees. There are notices that must be posted, policies you must have on hand, trainings that have to be given and documented, and more. Many of these are industry-specific. It is recommended to join your local association for your industry. If there isn't one locally, join a state or a national association. They usually have resources to help you stay in compliance.

Many times, your insurance agent can help you to know what policies you need to have. There will be many related to safety, non-discrimination, hiring and firing practices, etc. A company handbook is a must and should include all of your work rules and policies. Update it annually and have your staff sign that they received a copy and understand its contents.

Choose Your Vendors

When choosing vendors, it is a good idea to get references. Unless they are your only choice (for example, the water and sewer, electric, etc.), you can get other people's opinions of the services and products they offer. These days there are a lot of variables to consider. Do they have good prices? Good quality? How quickly can they deliver? Do they offer credit or only immediate payment?

In the past, you could be stuck using the only supplier in town. Now that there are so many delivery services and options to order online, you can negotiate to get the best prices. Buying local is still great but remember you must stay profitable! You are the only one responsible for the health of your business, so remember you must make hard choices sometimes to stay open. That could mean saving money and choosing another vendor.

Branding

When you are in the conceptual stage of starting your business, you really need to think about what image you want to have. Branding is extremely important! You do not need to have a ton of marketing materials on hand, but you should invest in a good logo. You can spend as little as $5 to several hundred or thousands of dollars on a professional logo on websites like fiverr.com. Once you have a logo, you can design your space and marketing materials around it.

Your brand should reflect the experience that you want your customer to have. For example, if you are a food truck whose target market is college students; you may want a more playful logo and branding. If your target market is high-end weddings, you will want an elegant logo and brand.

You also want to set yourself apart with your brand. If the other food truck in town has a taco logo, do not do a variation of it. Find something completely different, with completely different colors. You want to have a unique feel to your brand so that it is a new and exciting feeling that creates buzz.

Mascots are fun and memorable. Think of Geico and Bounty paper towels. Their mascots come to mind immediately, right? Look through some mascot ideas online and consider adopting one for your business.

Now that you have a menu, it's also important that you make your truck stand out from the rest. You can do this by means of aesthetics. While some people say that food is the only important thing in any food business, you know for a fact that it isn't true. Of course, it's also important for customers to be able to eat somewhere nice because no one really wants to eat in a truck that's rusty or that's not even designed at all. If you don't have time to set up your truck in such a way that it would attract people, it may also mean that you are not yet ready for this business and that you may have to really think things through.

Anyway, there are some things that you have to keep in mind when it comes to designing and decorating your food truck. These things are:

1. **The Theme:** Suppose you're creating a burger business, it won't be right to use pastels as the theme or put photos of classic Hollywood stars on the walls of your truck, would it?

You have to make sure that the theme you choose is connected to what you're serving so that your customers won't be confused.

2. **Color Scheme:** The main rule is to use the colors on the opposing sides of the color wheel. This way, everything will go together and your truck won't look like it's painted by a two-year-old. Also, it would be nice if the color scheme of your truck is also something you can use for the uniforms of you and your staff to make everything cohesive.

3. **Seats:** Some food trucks actually allow their customers to sit around the truck so if you can put out some chairs or anything that your customers can sit on, that would be good.

4. **Utensils and Packaging:** It would also be nice if you could set up the truck in such a way that your customers won't have a hard time getting the utensils that they need. Always keep condiments and tissues around because most customers need them, and make sure that you have environment-friendly bags that they can just pick up and put their orders in so they can take them on the go.

5. **And Of Course, Give It Some Life:** The best thing that you can do with your truck is to put some of your personality in it. This way, you're truck won't be generic and when people see it, they'll be excited to eat. When people notice that a food truck has life and that it's something cool, chances are they'll really go on and try your products, and that's something that's definitely good for you!

Attract customers and they certainly will eat what you have prepared! Let your truck speak for itself.

CHAPTER 10:

Getting Ready For Inspection

If your food operation cannot pass a food inspection by the Health Department you will not serve food to the public and make money. Please keep in mind, not all of the items we will cover may apply for your state inspector; however, you will have a strong working knowledge of the expectations your business will need to achieve to prepare for inspection.

Here, we will cover the:

- The Purpose of Health Inspectors

- Types of Inspections

- What Inspectors Look for

- Food Inspection Examples

The Purpose of Health Inspectors

A Health Inspector's sole purpose is to protect the public from food-borne illness. Hence, they are verifying that your business operation has good retail practices that exercise preventative measures to control pathogens, chemicals, and physical objects into foods prepared for consumption by the public.

Types of Inspections

Three types of inspections will be conducted by the Health Department:

- Pre-Inspection Prior to Opening

- Periodic No-Notice Food Inspections

- Temporary Event Inspections

A pre-inspection conducted by the Health Department prior to a food truck opening for operation and a periodic no-notice food inspection are the same types of inspection, with one exception. Periodic no-notice food inspections are used to observe you performing safe food handling practices while serving the public.

Temporary event inspections are food inspections conducted by the health department for events lasting 14-days in duration or less. Check with your county health department for the procedures required to serve food in this capacity.

What do inspectors look for? Health inspectors are inspecting your commercial kitchen or commissary, and your food truck for organization and process application. An inspector shared with me that a health inspector can make a determination of whether or not you have your stuff together by doing a 5-second observation of how you are organized. Specifically:

- Is your food permit properly displayed?

- Is your food truck clean?

- Do you know where your food thermometer is located?

- Do you know where your test strips for verifying if the sanitization of water is made properly, located?

- Are you wearing an Apron and single-used gloves while handling food?

- Do you have a Wash (Green Bucket) and a Sanitizer (Red Bucket) filled with water?

- Is food stored on your truck 6 inches off the floor?

Most of these items are common sense, but you would be surprised how uncommon these things are to food truck operators that do not have a clue what they are doing.

Basic Inspection Guidelines

Commercial Kitchen or Commissary

- Hand washing Sink
  - Hot/cold water dispenses
  - Soap dispenser present & operational
  - Paper towels present
- Toilet Facilities
  - Self-closing restroom doors
  - Paper towels present
  - Soap dispenser present & operational
- Trash Cans
  - Clean with trash bags

- Lids that cover the can
- Ware washing
  - A 3-compartment sink present
  - Wash, Rinse, Sanitize
  - Test strips are present
- Food Contact Surfaces
  - Surfaces are non-porous
  - Cleaning solution available to clean surfaces

Good Food Practices

- No bare hand contact with ready to eat food
- Wash hands in the hand sink, not in the dishwater sink
- Use single-use gloves
- Cook foods to the proper temperature
  - 165 °F for raw poultry
  - 155 °F for ground beef, ground pork, shell eggs
  - 145 °F for beef, pork, lamb, seafood
    - Chemical Supplies
  - Use only approved food grade chemicals
  - Never store the food product together with the chemical product
  - Label all chemical containers
    - Store dry food goods 6 inches or more off the ground

Food Safety Knowledge

- Time & Temperature Principles
  - A 41 °F-135 °F range, where bacteria grows rapidly
- Metal Stem Thermometers
  - Must be food grade (NSF)
  - Know how to calibrate
- Holding Food for Serving
  - Minimum hot holding temperature 135 °F
  - Minimum cold holding temperature 41 °F
- Reheating Food to Serve
  - Reheat to 165 °F
  - Reheat rapidly for 2 hrs. or less
  - Reheat only once
- Employees that are ill can contaminate food; send them home if they are ill
- Clean and sanitize all utensils and surfaces that touch the food

Know how to make sanitization water with bleach or QUAT (Ammonia). Food truck operators are required to have test strips available to ensure the proper ratio of water and bleach, or the QUAT solution is prepared correctly to effectively sanitize utensils and cookware.

Food truck operators also need to have proper cleaning buckets present to regularly clean food contact surfaces. Check with your local food equipment supplier for a green bucket and a red bucket cleaning and sanitizer combo. The green bucket will contain a cleaning solution consistent with soap water and the red bucket will contain a sanitizer solution consistent with chlorine (bleach) or QUAT.

When cleaning food contact surfaces, wipe down the surface with a cleaning rag submersed in the green bucket and sanitize the food contact surface with the same cleaning rag after it is submerged in the red bucket. After you have cleaned the food contact surface, keep the cleaning rag in the red bucket, which contains the sanitizer solution. Always, Always, replenish these buckets with fresh water during a given food shift operation. I typically will change the water every 2-3 hours during a 10-hour shift.

Sample Food Inspection

INSPECTIONS & APPEALS

Food Establishment Inspection Report

Food and Consumer Safety BureauDepartment of Inspections & Appeals	No. Of Risk Factor/Intervention Violations	0	Date: Ommitted
Food and Consumer Safety Bureau			Time In: 5:48 PM
321 E 13th ST FL 3	No. Of Repeat Factor/Intervention Violations	0	Time Out:5:49 PM
Des Moines, IA 50319-0083			

| Establishment: HUT 1 HUT FOOD | Address: Hidden For Privacy | City/State: Bellevue, NE | Zip: 68123 | | Telephone: Hidden For Privacy |
| License/Permit#: 94467 - Mobile Food Unit License | Permit Holder: HUT 1 HUT FOOD TRUCK, LLC | Inspection Reason: Routine | Est. Type: Temporary/Food, Mobile Food Unit | Risk Category: Risk Level 4 (High) |

FOODBORNE ILLNESS RISK FACTORS AND PUBLIC HEALTH INTERVENTIONS

IN = In compliance   OUT = Not in compliance   N/O = Not observed   N/A = Not applicable   (*) = Corrected on site during inspection (COS)   R = Repeat violation

Supervision					
1. Person in charge present, demonstrates knowledge, and performs duties	IN		15. Food separated and protected (Cross Contamination and Environmental)	IN
2. Certified Food Protection Manager	IN		16. Food contact surfaces: cleaned and sanitized	IN
Employee Health			17. Proper disposition of returned, previously served, reconditioned, and unsafe food	IN
3. Management, food employee and conditional employee knowledge, responsibilities and reporting	IN		Potentially Hazardous Food Time/Temperature Control for Safety	
4. Proper use of exclusions and restrictions	IN		18. Proper cooking time and temperatures	IN
5. Procedures for responding to vomiting and diarrheal events	IN		19. Proper reheating procedures of hot holding	IN
Good Hygienic Practices			20. Proper cooling time and temperatures	N/O
6. Proper eating, tasting, drinking, or tobacco use	IN		21. Proper hot holding temperatures	IN
7. No discharge from eyes, nose, and mouth	IN		22. Proper cold holding temperatures	IN
Control of Hands as a Vehicle of Contamination			23. Proper date marking and disposition	IN
8. Hands clean and properly washed	IN		24. Time as a public health control: procedures and records	N/A
9. No bare hand contact with ready to eat foods	IN		Consumer Advisory	
10. Hand washing sinks properly supplied and accessible	IN		25. Consumer advisory provided for raw or undercooked foods	N/A
Approved Source			Highly Susceptible Populations	
11. Foods obtained from an approved source	IN		26. Pasteurized foods used; prohibited foods not offered	N/A
12. Foods received at proper temperatures	N/O		Food/Color Additives and Toxic Substances	
13. Food in good condition, safe, and unadulterated	IN		27. Food additives: approved, properly stored, and used	N/A
14. Required records available; shellstock tags, parasite destruction	N/A		28. Toxic substances properly identified, stored and used	IN
Protection from Contamination			Conformance with Approved Procedures	
			29. Compliance with variance, specialized process, reduced oxygen packaging criteria, and HACCP plan	N/A

GOOD RETAIL PRACTICES
Good Retail Practices are preventative measures to control the addition of pathogens, chemicals, and physical objects into foods.

Safe Food and Water			Proper Use of Utensils	
30. Pasteurized eggs used where required	N/A		43. In use utensils: properly stored	IN
31. Water and ice from approved source	IN		44. Utensils, equipment, and linens: properly stored dried and handled	IN
32. Variance obtained for specialized processing methods	N/A		45. Single-use/single service articles: properly stored and used	IN
Food Temperature Control			46. Slash-resistant and cloth glove use	N/A
33. Proper cooling methods used; adequate equipment for temperature control	IN		Utensils, Equipment, and Vending	
34. Plant food properly cooked for hot holding	IN		47. Food and non-food contact surfaces are cleanable, properly designed, constructed, and used	IN
35. Approved thawing methods	IN		48. Warewashing facilities: installed, maintained, and used; test strips	IN
36. Thermometers provided and accurate	IN		49. Non-food contact surfaces clean	IN
Food Identification			Physical Facilities	
37. Food properly labeled; original container	IN		50. Hot and Cold water available, adequate pressure	IN
Prevention of Food Contamination			51. Plumbing installed; proper backflow devices	IN
38. Insects, rodents, and animals not present/outer openings protected	IN		52. Sewage and waste water properly disposed	IN
39. Contamination prevented during food preparation, storage and display	IN		53. Toilet facilities: properly constructed, supplied, and cleaned	IN
40. Personal cleanliness	IN		54. Garbage and refuse properly disposed; facilities maintained	IN
41. Wiping cloths: properly used and stored	IN		55. Physical facilities installed, maintained, and clean	IN
42. Washing fruits and vegetables	N/A		56. Adequate ventilation and lighting; designated areas used	IN
			57. Licensing; posting licenses and reports; smoking	IN

Food Establishment Inspection Report

Food and Consumer Safety Bureau Department of Inspections & Appeals Food and Consumer Safety Bureau 321 E 12th ST FL 3 Des Moines, IA 50319-0083	No. Of Risk Factor/Intervention Violations	0	Date: Ommitted Time In: 5:48 PM		
	No. Of Repeat Factor/Intervention Violations	0	Time Out: 5:49 PM		
Establishment: HUT 1 HUT FOOD	Address: Hidden For Privacy	City/State: Bellevue, NE	Zip: 68123		Telephone: Hidden For Privacy
License/Permit#: 94467 - Mobile Food Unit License	Permit Holder: HUT 1 HUT FOOD TRUCK, LLC	Inspection Reason: Routine	Est. Type: Temporary/Food, Mobile Food Unit		Risk Category: Risk Level 4 (High)

FOODBORNE ILLNESS RISK FACTORS AND PUBLIC HEALTH INTERVENTIONS

IN = In compliance OUT = Not in compliance N/O = Not observed N/A = Not applicable   (*) = Corrected on site during inspection (COS) R = Repeat violation

Supervision			15. Food separated and protected (Cross Contamination and Environmental)		IN
1. Person in charge present, demonstrates knowledge, and performs duties	IN		16. Food contact surfaces: cleaned and sanitized		IN
2. Certified Food Protection Manager	IN		17. Proper disposition of returned, previously served, reconditioned, and unsafe food		IN
Employee Health			**Potentially Hazardous Food Time/Temperature Control for Safety**		
3. Management, food employee and conditional employee knowledge, responsibilities and reporting	IN		18. Proper cooking time and temperatures		IN
4. Proper use of exclusions and restrictions	IN		19. Proper reheating procedures of hot holding		IN
5. Procedures for responding to vomiting and diarrheal events	IN		20. Proper cooling time and temperatures		N/O
Good Hygienic Practices			21. Proper hot holding temperatures		IN
6. Proper eating, tasting, drinking, or tobacco use	IN		22. Proper cold holding temperatures		IN
7. No discharge from eyes, nose, and mouth	IN		23. Proper date marking and disposition		IN
Control of Hands as a Vehicle of Contamination			24. Time as a public health control: procedures and records		N/A
8. Hands clean and properly washed	IN		**Consumer Advisory**		
9. No bare hand contact with ready to eat foods	IN		25. Consumer advisory provided for raw or undercooked foods		N/A
10. Hand washing sinks properly supplied and accessible	IN		**Highly Susceptible Populations**		
Approved Source			26. Pasteurized foods used: prohibited foods not offered		N/A
11. Foods obtained from an approved source	IN		**Food/Color Additives and Toxic Substances**		
12. Foods received at proper temperatures	N/O		27. Food additives: approved, properly stored, and used		N/A
13. Food in good condition, safe, and unadulterated	IN		28. Toxic substances properly identified, stored and used		IN
14. Required records available, shellstock tags, parasite destruction	N/A		**Conformance with Approved Procedures**		
Protection from Contamination			29. Compliance with variance, specialized process, reduced oxygen packaging criteria, and HACCP plan		N/A

GOOD RETAIL PRACTICES
Good Retail Practices are preventative measures to control the addition of pathogens, chemicals, and physical objects into foods.

Safe Food and Water			**Proper Use of Utensils**	
30. Pasteurized eggs used where required	N/A		43. In use utensils: properly stored	IN
31. Water and ice from approved source	IN		44. Utensils, equipment, and linens: properly stored, dried and handled	IN
32. Variance obtained for specialized processing methods	N/A		45. Single-use/single service articles: properly stored and used	IN
Food Temperature Control			46. Slash-resistant and cloth glove use	N/A
33. Proper cooling methods used; adequate equipment for temperature control	IN		**Utensils, Equipment, and Vending**	
34. Plant food properly cooked for hot holding	IN		47. Food and non-food contact surfaces are cleanable, properly designed, constructed, and used	IN
35. Approved thawing methods	IN		48. Warewashing facilities: installed, maintained, and used; test strips	IN
36. Thermometers provided and accurate	IN		49. Non-food contact surfaces clean	IN
Food Identification			**Physical Facilities**	
37. Food properly labeled; original container	IN		50. Hot and Cold water available; adequate pressure	IN
Prevention of Food Contamination			51. Plumbing installed; proper backflow devices	IN
38. Insects, rodents, and animals not present/outer openings protected	IN		52. Sewage and waste water properly disposed	IN
39. Contamination prevented during food preparation, storage and display	IN		53. Toilet facilities: properly constructed, supplied, and cleaned	IN
40. Personal cleanliness	IN		54. Garbage and refuse properly disposed; facilities maintained	IN
41. Wiping cloths: properly used and stored	IN		55. Physical facilities installed, maintained, and clean	IN
42. Washing fruits and vegetables	N/A		56. Adequate ventilation and lighting; designated areas used	IN
			57. Licensing, posting licenses and reports; smoking	IN

Inspection reports shall be posted no higher than eye level where the public can see and in a manner that the public can reasonably read the report

P - Priority   PF- Priority Foundation   C - Core

FOODBORNE ILLNESS RISK FACTORS AND PUBLIC HEALTH INTERVENTIONS				
Item Number	Violation of Code	Priority Level	Comment	Correct By Date

| GOOD RETAIL PRACTICES | | | | |
Good Retail Practices are preventative measures to control the addition of pathogens, chemicals, and physical objects into foods.				
Item Number	Violation of Code	Priority Level	Comment	Correct By Date

Inspection Published Comment:
Routine inspection done as followup to new mobile unit, Hut 1 Hut.

The following guidance documents have been issued:

Hidden for privacy

Jeff Fulson
Person In Charge

Hidden for privacy

Tenesha Stubblefield
Inspector

Inspection reports shall be posted no higher than eye level where the public can see and in a manner that the public can reasonably read the report

P - Priority   PF- Priority Foundation   C - Core

FOODBORNE ILLNESS RISK FACTORS AND PUBLIC HEALTH INTERVENTIONS				
Item Number	Violation of Code	Priority Level	Comment	Correct By Date

| GOOD RETAIL PRACTICES | | | | |
Good Retail Practices are preventative measures to control the addition of pathogens, chemicals, and physical objects into foods.				
Item Number	Violation of Code	Priority Level	Comment	Correct By Date

Inspection Published Comment:
Routine inspection done as followup to new mobile unit, Hut 1 Hut.

The following guidance documents have been issued:

Hidden for privacy

Jeff Fulson
Person In Charge

Hidden for privacy

Tenesha Stubblefield
Inspector

Visit food.iowa.gov

CHAPTER 11:

Mission, Vision, and Goals

VISION

Offer wonderful eating experience with great food at reasonable prices.

MISSION

"Serve the highest levels of experiential product and services and maintain consistency in serving the highest quality products at affordable price"

Before you start your business plan, you should identify what your mission, vision, and goals are. They should explain why you are in business and what you hope to accomplish. They are also guideposts when things get difficult. Below we will discuss developing each part.

A mission statement is a short statement that is specific and defines your purpose. It should be inspiring as well as engaging and customer-focused. An example is: *"We believe in high quality and delicious food. In order to serve our customers well, we are constantly trying new recipes to inspire new flavors and create new trends."*

A vision statement is a short statement about your big dream and vision for the company. The key is to project where you want to be in ten years but uses the present tense. For example: *"ABC Food Truck is the premiere food truck in Entrepreneur City, serving events of all sizes."*

Goals are very important and should be reviewed and updated on a regular basis. Some people even write goals daily. It is a good idea to write SMART goals. SMART goals are an acronym for Specific, Measurable, Achievable, Relevant, and Time-Based.

To be specific, include the who, what, where, when, why, and how. Define exactly what it is that you want to accomplish.

In order for your goal to be measurable, you have to be able to track progress and have a data point to know when you have accomplished your goal. For example, when a non-profit is raising money, it is easy to track progress by the amount of money they have raised.

Making your goal achievable is important because you want to be sure it is reasonable. If you set your goals too high, you could get discouraged easily. If you set it too low, you could set yourself up for failure by becoming bored.

Making your goal relevant is important because it needs to be worthwhile and meet your needs. Also, when writing multiple goals, be sure they complement each other and are not repetitive.

Lastly, give your goal a time frame. This will create a structure and keep you working towards the goal with a sense of urgency.

An example of a SMART goal is: *"ABC Food Truck will book at least 3 events each week and will have next year booked by July of this year totaling 75 events."*

If you have a large goal, such as 75 events booked in 6 months, break it down into smaller pieces with smaller time frames. *'3 events per week'* seems much more doable than 75 events in 6 months.

Another idea is to set a goal for each quarter of the year, pushing your personal limits each time. With a shorter time frame, it is easier to not burn out on your goal when you meet challenges. Sometimes setting daily goals is best, especially when things feel overwhelming.

Whatever you choose, setting goals is vital. Set yourself up for success!

Conclusion

A food truck business can be very lucrative because there are a lot of people who frequently eat at mobile restaurants. Rather than waiting for customers to get to your store, you can go where they are and attract them with a special assortment of delicious dishes.

You can start and operate a food truck business with far fewer staff than it would need to operate a standard restaurant. This is also less demanding and requires lower operating costs compared to a conventional restaurant business.

You should start by having a clear business plan. In terms of the dishes served and the customers you want to attract, you need to pick the exact niche in the food industry. As most aspects of your business rely on these variables, you need to pick them from the very beginning. If you want to sell fast food, soups, pastries, ice creams, or multi-cooking meals, you need to learn.

You do need to know the age group you'd be targeting, whether they are teenagers, teens, college students, executives, or senior citizens. While the age ranges would overlap, you need to keep your target clients in mind before starting your business.

You do have to keep in mind a particular target for your business. What's your business going to be for the next five or ten years? How many more trucks and workers would you have been using by then? What kind of income do you expect to earn in the future? These are some of the goals you need to set very early on for your business.

Once you have a clear picture of what you plan to do, you can obtain the necessary licenses and permits for your business. You do need to be mindful that some towns and cities do not permit you to operate a food truck business. And you have to select your place of business based on the laws in force in the area.

If you have the permits, you need to buy your business a food truck. You may purchase a new or used vehicle, or hire or even loan one for a certain amount of time. If you need financing for your business, you may need to find an appropriate bank or a private investor.

Once you have all of these in place, you can immediately start running your business. The secret of being successful in the mobile food business is being unique and offering something that no one else can offer. People still look for novelty and variety. You will become competitive in the food truck business if you can deliver what they want.

FOOD TRUCK BUSINESS STRATEGIES

TURN YOUR PASSION INTO PROFIT BY STARTING YOUR OWN MOBILE FOOD TRUCK BUSINESS AND LEARN TIPS ON HOW TO MANAGE AND INCREASE YOUR SALES

RYAN BOURDAIN

DONALD MURPHY

Introduction

Starting your own business is not an easy task! It doesn't matter if it is a large or small business; there will always be roadblocks and challenges to be faced along the way. Brick and mortar businesses have been around for a long time and have developed well-established procedures for others to follow. If you are opening a physical restaurant, there's a good chance you can easily find someone to help you navigate through your journey.

But what if your business is mobile and is set to operate in multiple areas, cities, counties, and regions? In this case, there are fewer proven strategies and procedures to follow. The freedom to roam around with your business is littered with challenges... most of which are unique to almost every truck. Being in a new place each and every day can wear on almost any food truck owner. From health codes to inventory management to budgets, you've got to have a strong will to survive in this type of business.

From the viewpoint of an outsider, the food truck business appears to be a lot of fun! And this is what is typically perceived by onlookers and customers thinking about starting their food truck. What isn't necessarily visible on the surface is all the hard work that goes into getting the truck up and running, setting up a profitable menu, marketing, pricing, mechanical maintenance, adhering to regulations, staffing, and much more!

Running your own food truck business requires more than just a passion for preparing and serving great food! It takes a lot of research and planning before a single penny is spent for the purchase of an actual food truck. Composing a detailed business plan is essential in the early stages. Even with a sound business plan in place, don't be surprised if things get more expensive than you originally budgeted in the startup phase. That is a sentiment shared by many food truck owners.

In today's world, there is a new trend of street food connoisseurs invading the new hot spot, food truck, food festival, or that little mobile food court on the corner. Although food businesses are not a new concept for entrepreneurs and consumers, it is one of the preferred activities of young adults and 20 something-year-olds. This generation is increasing year over year, and will be, if it already isn't, the biggest age-pool of customers in the world population.

These food lovers are always on the hunt for the newest food and beverage mix, trendy hotspot, or that iconic favorite that they can tell everyone they know about. All food businesses, whether a brick & mortar location, mobile business, booth, etc. must be aware not only of what the trends are but also must be aware of the legislation regarding food safety. As a business owner, you are ultimately responsible for ensuring that the food you are serving is well received and safe.

Food truck businesses are increasing partly due to the economic fluctuations in the past several years. There is a sudden upsurge trend that has started off, with consumers seeking inexpensive meal options that can be served in short amount of time. Although in the beginning, this had a slight effect on food-based businesses that are brick and mortar based, restauranteurs were quick to add on food trucks as part of a new revenue stream.

From an entrepreneurial standpoint, food trucks, mobile food businesses, and booths/cart setups have lower overhead expenses than restaurants and can easily relocate to pursue new revenue streams if needed.

From a consumer perspective, there is something amazing about not having to commute to get good food when the food will now come to you at lesser cost. There are a variety of options for those who want to start a food business:

- Restaurant

- Full Service

- Quick Service

- Delivery

- Retail Location

- Shop

- Farmers Market

- Concessions

- Wholesale

- Boutiques

- Big Box Stores

But first, let us talk about the misconceptions of owning a business and the common mistakes aspiring entrepreneurs make before they even get their business off the ground.

These assumptions and mistakes are typically facts and suggestions everyone hears from their peers without really looking into what is being told. These suggestions lead to false assumptions about what having a business is like, what it will involve, and how much money can be made. Most of the assumptions an aspiring entrepreneur has are usually unrealistic. Having unrealistic assumptions about owning a business usually leads to wrong strategies for the business, which in turn creates uncontrollable problems, causing business failure.

CHAPTER 1:

Who Stops at Food Carts?

....for the people eating at these carts, never appear to grow old. That is because people genuinely appreciate getting those special foods at the festival like southern style doughnuts or cinnamon almonds. These are special treats that the old and youthful alike can't leave behind when they land at a fair. Be that as it may, at that point you have the food trucks that are perched on ordinary streets, the ones that offer healthy foods to grown-ups searching for a snappy lunch on their way back to work. These trucks are excellent too because the food they offer is modest and quick. Numerous business people stop at food trucks each day and increasingly more people appear to pick this lunch alternative regularly.

If you need to start up your own business yet aren't sure what to get into, take a gander at these versatile kitchens. If you've generally longed for having your eatery, however, are frightened by the cost and duty required, then food trucks can be a venturing stone as they get you into the food-service industry for lower speculation and you can fabricate a name and notoriety for yourself and your product. At that point the progression to an out and out retail facade café can be more straightforward. Food trucks are moderately easy to begin and they're mainstream for new business owners as well as for the overall population also. Numerous food truck owners love running it and the fact that everybody around appreciate and patronize them for some excellent quality food, at reasonable costs and quick service. It's undoubtedly a win-win for everybody included. Be that as it may, in case you are as yet not persuaded there's still more to this story.

Food carts are unique. For people who live in enormous urban communities, they may turn out to be simply one more piece of the scene (even though that doesn't stop them from eating at them frequently). However, for people who aren't used to the vast city the idea of eating at a food cart is fascinating, new and unique. These people couldn't care less that the food you are serving isn't gourmet (in spite of the fact that you'd be astonished at the assortment of food types accessible from portable food vendors nowadays), all they need is to give it a shot since that is the thing that 'enormous city people' do. So, there's dependably another person willing to attempt what you bring to the table.

The Freedom to Move

Another great thing about food carts as a business is that they can be on the move. With a physical customer facing facade, you are tied down to that place. If you pick a place and it ends up being dead space where nobody goes, then you are doomed, thanks to it. A food cart allows you to move around and go any place you please (inside the guidelines, obviously!). So, if one day you are on a street corner that doesn't have much business, the following day you can move elsewhere. If you start on one street; however, it starts to get exhausting you can move along from that point too. You can even be a portable street cart that moves around throughout the day.

The beginning is easy with the right data, making a profit is altogether attainable if you've set yourself upright and you never need to stress over running out of people to serve or getting exhausted with the view. Since there's less hazard in a portable food vending business than numerous different types of private ventures, you and your new food cart can be set for a great start right from the earliest starting point.

CHAPTER 2:

What Is Cheaper to Run, A Restaurant, or A Food Truck?

Which of the two are more environmentally friendly or economical to operate or is there no conclusive answer? At present, numerous people may rapidly accept that food trucks are the more regrettable of the two evils of the national focus on how naturally economical practices tie to methods of transportation.

However, sustainability is something that becomes an integral factor at whatever point a light is turned on, plastic is tossed into the trash, dishes are washed, and so forth. Environmentally friendly (or destructive) practices don't begin and stop with the key in the ignition; however, they rather occur during and after every single working hour of a business -- in a food trailer or in a customary physical café.

How about we take a look at the components that become possibly the most important factors during these business tasks.

The location: As you most likely are aware, catering trucks are mobile. They move all around and subsequently leave a smaller impression on where they've been. There's little framework, besides the business kitchen, that should be kept up. And then, there are eateries. Cafés have numerous huge areas that must be lit up, cleaned regularly, and temperature regulated. These physical elements exist constantly, not simply during working hours.

Energy Use: As referenced above, a conventional café's physical area makes the requirement for electricity and natural gas to keep up comfortable temperatures and to give light to eating clients. In the kitchens, cooking is commonly done with natural gas and frying pans and stoves are kept hot during the working hours. As per the 2003 Commercial Building Energy Consumption Survey, most eateries utilize 38.4kWh of electricity per square foot every year, which is roughly 77,000 kWh every year for a 2,000 sq. ft. eatery.

Food trucks likewise require a heat source for cooking, so they commonly use propane. During a year, a normal food trailer will utilize around 900 gallons of propane, in addition to fuel prerequisites for driving around. In spite of the fact that this fuel is generally diesel or gas, catering trucks may likewise utilize biodiesel or vegetable oil. Besides, an onboard generator addresses the electricity issue. While generators are normally more polluting than grid-provided power, food trailers demand less power and depend more on natural light.

Vehicle miles: Although restaurants can't pile on miles going to clients, their clients are most likely traveling to get to these customary eateries. A short outing by a food truck can frequently counterbalance various little excursions by clients that would have generally driven to an eatery.

Waste: For the waste component in the food business, it's a tie between food trucks and eateries. While some catering trucks are considered eco-friendly by utilizing corn-based plastic, bagasse, or reused paper takeout compartments, despite everything they're making squanders. Conversely, eateries can utilize reusable plates, cups, and utensils; be that as it may, take-out and fast-food eateries frequently depend vigorously on take-out containers that are made of Styrofoam and plastic.

Is the winner clear yet? From this subjective analysis, clearly, mobile food stands generally produce less hurtful ecological effects. It is completely conceivable that a few eateries will be more sustainable than other food trailers.

Keep in mind, as a food truck proprietor you should pay attention to your clients' interests. Your enthusiasm for ecological practices will hold steadfast followers and pull in new clients to your business.

Pros of Food Trucking

- Money! And loads of it. Regardless of whether you need two or three hundred dollars per week, several hundred a day, or a couple hundred per hour... these are for the most part realistic figures in mobile concessions.

- Freedom! You make your very own hours. Work 1 day a week or work 7 days every week. Take a multi-week excursion at whatever point you need. It's up to you. You are the chief. This can also be perilous. So, if you aren't spurred, this isn't for you. You will wind up with a costly residue collector in your carport.

- You can begin with next to zero cash.

- No nagging boss or corporate structure.

Cons of Food Trucking

- This is work, it is difficult to work and extended periods of time.

- Obtaining licenses.

- Learning and following the city and state guidelines.

- Obtaining insurance, license, and a commissary.

- Inventory and prep work.

- The daily tidying up.

- Working around extraordinary climate or finding shielded zones.

CHAPTER 3:

Drafting the Business Plan

After you and your partners have decided on what roles to play and how to split the profits, the next thing to do is to draft the business plan. This is the stage where the big idea will begin to take shape. We will go over some of the important points that you will need for your business plan and then we will take a look at an example of an actual business plan but first, why do you need one?

What is a business plan and why is it required?

Business plans are required if you are seeking third-party capital from banks, the small business administration, or other lenders. Even if you are not required to put one together to get such financing, the initial preparation and planning are critical to the success of your business and will likely help you avoid costly mistakes.

If partners are involved the business plan is even more important to ensure the alignment of vision, necessary to avoid later disputes that can threaten the survival of the business.

Points to Ponder in The Planning of Food Truck Business

Certain items unique to the food truck business should be included in your planning such as:

The Local Food Truck Marketplace

The Market Analysis portion of the business plan is one of the hardest to make since it takes a lot of objective data gathered from the research of both primary and secondary sources.

In this case, we are interested in opening up a food truck business. Some industry research and statistics may be called for but the best research will be familiarizing yourself with local brands. This means internet research on the kinds of food trucks in your area (to help with differentiation and branding).

It also makes sense to look for "food truck lots." Many cities have parking lots that are leased or used by a collection of trucks for the business lunch crowd. In many cases, food trucks are parked here permanently and have a predictability that many food truck businesses lack. This may be the safest place to start your new business because you will have documented foot traffic, predictable food costs, and relatively consistent sales, which are rare in the industry. The potential downside here is that your brand will need to be materially different than the offerings from the other trucks.

It also makes sense to research the annual local fairs, festivals, and events within 50 miles of your home base. This information is easy to find online and organizers are often very happy to give you attendance and exhibitor cost information because they want you there. This information can help you project costs and illustrate to potential investors where you plan to seek revenue in building your business.

Understanding the Competition

Once you have worked through the local market, you will need to isolate the trucks that are either in direct or indirect competition with the truck you have conceived. *Direct competition* would be a substantially similar menu offering to the one you have in mind and you would want to make sure that you are not setting yourself up to compete with an established brand in a narrow marketplace. *Indirect competition* would be some overlap in the menu but sufficient difference in offerings that clients would conceivably be attracted to both businesses independently, were they to be at the same venue. Adjusting your menu may be a way to reduce concerns that arise from the direct and indirect competition.

Differentiation in the brand and product offering is critical to food truck success and should be a huge part of your business plan. This doesn't mean you shouldn't start a food truck that is similar to another in the area but it does mean that you should do so only after working out how you plan to compete with that truck. The strategy for success, however, is often more complicated than that.

Will you offer better quality food, a larger menu, longer service hours, or a better price? Perhaps some combination of these?

Business Strategy

In planning the business strategy, there are four basic business approaches that you can use to increase the likelihood of success for your business. These are cost leadership, differentiation, location, and hybrid.

Cost Leadership Strategy

This is very often the first strategy a new business seeks and it can be a devastatingly bad one. Frankly, it should only be considered in a rare set of circumstances. Specifically, this should only be considered for a very generic food offering in a high traffic environment. For example, if you are selling hot dogs, hamburgers, or fries at a state fair and can move tremendous volume, reasonable profit is still possible. To compete with this strategy, extra research is required to get the lowest possible food cost at a quality you can live with. Do not think that you will build a repeat following simply by being cheap. In fact, if not careful, you may send the message that your food is lower quality or less desirable to attract clients at a low cost.

Differentiation Strategy

The next strategy and one which more often makes sense is differentiation. As the name implies, the differentiation strategy would position your food truck in such a way that only you sell unique food products. Whether they are secret family recipes, hard to find food products, or creative dishes, these products set you apart because they cannot be offered by others. Quality is critical in the differentiation strategy but if the food is great and hard to find, your brand can achieve margins that are much more generous, leading to higher profits with lower sales and effort. This not only impacts the overall value of your business; it means a higher return on investment across the board.

Location Strategy

This can be a very effective strategy, especially at the start of the food truck for ensuring a solid, even loyal customer base. An example of this can be found with a truck owner we know in Los Angeles. He learned that a local clothing manufacturer had hundreds of employees, many of whom did not drive cars. He asked the owner of the company if he could serve breakfast and lunch to those employees and remit a small percentage of profits to the company for the right to set up there. The truck took off and is now permanently located there, with another truck purchased in a matter of a few months to grow the business. If you are aware of an area that is underserved by local restaurants or loaded with employees who cannot conveniently leave for lunch, this strategy can be very effective.

Hybrid Strategy

This strategy uses some combination of the above approaches to maximize the success of the truck. For example, we know of trucks that are in a particular place every Monday and another on Tuesday, etc. The scarcity created for customers when they know if they want that item for lunch, they have to get it on a certain day can increase brand loyalty. This approach would combine both location and differentiation while getting the extra benefit of spreading awareness of the brand. Others might have a different menu offering for festivals or particularly high traffic events to take advantage of cost leverage strategy while maintaining differentiation through a select offering of exclusive popular dishes.

Food Pricing

One of the hardest and perhaps most important parts of putting together a business plan is to decide on the pricing of the product. In the case of food trucks, there are methods and strategies on how to properly price your dishes so that they can appeal to your target market and also get to a good profit. Pricing should be based on the cost of the raw materials that were used to make the dish.

Typically, most food establishments would set their pricing at between 35 to 45 percent markup of the dish's cost, which would include the food and the plate, fork, garnishes, etc. So, let's say that you are serving a dish with ingredients that reach up to a total of $5. You may make it have a selling price of $7.25. You can experiment with price. Exclusivity can drive costs up. For example, baseball stadiums can often charge $6 for a $2 hot dog, because they have exclusivity. Your lunch crowd weekday guests are going to be much more sensitive to price than attendees at a festival, where there is an expectation that prices will be higher on food. If you price your items too inexpensively, you may quickly learn that the message you send customers is that the food isn't very good. Experiment and you will find a comfortable range for each menu item.

If you are surrounded by other trucks, take the time to walk the grounds and get a sense of their offerings and prices. You don't want to charge $4 for a bottle of water when all others are charging $2.

Another important consideration in pricing your items is labor, both in preparation in the kitchen and at the time of service from the truck. If a particular item is more labor-intensive than others on your menu, you may reasonably adjust the price to reflect that. Failure to consider that can lead to a lack of profits that demotivates the owner and sabotages the chances of success for the truck.

Use of Strategic Partnerships

Strategic partnerships should also be considered in the planning of the business. There is an exceptionally successful lobster roll brand that relies on a family fishing connection to provide an inexpensive product, that can be marked up for a very nice margin. This is an example of a supplier strategic partnership that can provide a competitive advantage, which makes the business more attractive to financing and improves chances of success. Other examples of strategic partnerships might be favorable lease rates or exclusivity offered by a business owner or festival organizer, with whom you share a small piece of the profit. It is worth your time to consider who you know and how to leverage those relationships for competitive advantage.

Similarly, even if you don't have a supplier connection, you should spend a substantial amount of time interviewing and sampling food vendors to negotiate price, ensure product quality and keep your hard costs as low as possible. Your efforts in doing so should be documented in your business plan, to show your preparation for success, to those who may invest in your business.

As you become more established and work with various events, it is a good idea to keep up the relationships you had with organizers of previous events that you went to. Many organizers are in this business. They can give you advanced notice and great opportunities for good locations and events.

It also really pays to have partners who are in the media. Whether you donate to a cause that will be celebrated by the media or offer a strange food offering that is newsworthy, this kind of attention can make your brand explode. Many food trucks offer food challenges such as an 8-pound burrito that is free if it can be finished by two eaters in less than an hour. Not much exposure from cost standpoint but an interesting story and often news outlets love these angles of human interest to fill into the gaps on slow news days.

CHAPTER 4:

Financial Planning

What Numbers Should I Know?

"Know your numbers!" is a classic and overused phrase. However, it's vital to know your numbers—don't let the knowledge of them get away from you. Much stress and frustration can stem from the guessing game that ends up being played when you don't know your numbers.

You need to know how much money is coming in and going out every day, week, month, and year to know whether what you are doing is working. Knowing as much data as possible about your business will help take that guessing game off your plate and lighten the stress that comes with it.

The guessing game hurts you, your team, your business, and your customers. Once you know the basic numbers, you can start to dive in deeper. Then you can begin creating what I call "NextGen Numbers."

Later in this pin, I have included an extensive list of definitions and formulas on how to figure out those numbers.

Time to go beyond just knowing your numbers. Let's put them to work!

If you have your numbers in a program, it should be easy to break them down so you can see month-over-month and yearly trends. Utilizing these trends will help you get out of the guessing game and into making educated decisions based on the cold hard numbers, not what you feel.

Too often, people fall back into going with their gut feelings and what they knew to be true at one point in time. Things are changing every single day—in life and in business. It's imperative that you stay on top of the mounting trends in your business to avoid any blindside hits.

You can use the data you've collected to make investing in your business a lot simpler because you will know and not be guessing. Expanding and contracting areas of focus for your business will be leaps and bounds easier when you have the data laid out in front of you.

When was the last time you set sales goals for your business? You've heard that question before, I'm sure but I want you to take it one step further. Instead of just stating that you want to hit X sales goals for a period, track it and give periodic updates to your team based on the data available. That way your team can stay on task and on track to meet those goals. Tracking will also enable conversation on how to meet those goals. Without those conversations, you aren't giving your team a clear path to success, which is a quick way to wind up having unmet expectations and all-around disappointment.

Try to keep your goals obtainable and reasonable so you can use them as a springboard of encouragement for you and your team. Small wins are wins. You don't have to swing for the fences for a home run every time you go to set goals. Increases and decreases of 5 to 10 percent over specific periods of time should be reasonable. Setting such reasonable goals will also help with combating big downturns if you land the business that is a one-and-done deal. Next, we can move on to creating your own NextGen Numbers.

How Can I Create NextGen Numbers?

NextGen Numbers can be set for every position in your business and are different in every industry. They will help you track inefficiencies, which will save you money and add profit to your bottom line.

One example of a NextGen Number I created and used was to track the accuracy of our stock pickers in our central warehouse. Every day, hundreds of parts were picked off our central warehouse shelves to be sent to our satellite stores for stock and specific orders. We used a scanner and barcode system to create orders for the satellite stores that in theory should have been 100 percent accurate. As we quickly found out, that was far from the case.

Some members of our warehouse team were much more accurate in their scanning than others. The day after the inventory was sent, we would receive the corrections back. From there, I kept a running tally in a spreadsheet that gave team members a percentage score on their accuracy individually and as a whole. Based on this data, we determined we were able to lower our percentage of shipping errors out of our warehouse.

When it comes to figuring out what to track to base your NextGen Numbers on, you have to look at what data you have available to you. What data can you extract from the daily process you already have going on in your business? Once you decide what to track, you just need to keep a record of it in a spreadsheet. It doesn't need to be a super-complex spreadsheet but gather as many data points as possible to help you build an average and, most importantly, an expectation. Once you have that baseline of numbers, you can start to build an expectation and build predictions for how changes in your current process will affect the numbers. The results will most likely surprise you!

Once you have your basic numbers tracked and have goals built around them, you will be able to start finding and tracking these NextGen Numbers to start the process of building your business into a well-oiled machine.

Here's an outline of the basic numbers you should know to make educated decisions and help build your NextGen Numbers.

Expenses
Money spent in order to generate revenue.
Expense Target
The projected goal of the total expenses incurred during a specified time period.

Revenue
Income generated from sales.
Revenue Target
The projected goal of the total revenue during a specified time period.
Cost of Goods Sold
Cost of obtaining materials and creating the finished goods that are sold.
Formula: Beginning Merchandise Inventory + Net Purchases of Merchandise – Ending Merchandise Inventory

Profit
The surplus of money after total costs are deducted from total revenue.

Formula: (Revenue – Cost) / Revenue x 100

Profit Margin

Percentage of profit left after taxes.

Formula: After-Tax Profit x 100 / Cost of Sales

Net Profit

Total earned or lost in a specified time period. Formula: Total Expenses – Total Revenue

Gross Profit

Difference between revenue and cost of goods. Formula: Revenue – Total Expenses

Debt

Obligation to pay money.

Accounts Receivable

Amount of sales not yet paid for by customers.

Accounts Payable

Unpaid bills.

Return on Investment (ROI)

A percentage that compares profitability or efficiency of investments.

Formula: (Net Profit / Total Investment) x 100

Stock Turnover

The number of times inventory is replenished during a specific period.

Formula: Cost of Sales / Average Inventory

Sales

While it can be talked about as revenue, you should also know the number of units sold and the average number of transactions in a given period.

Sales Closing Rate

Percentage of prospects who become paying customers.

Formula: (Number of Successful Sales / Number of Leads) x 100

Average Time to Collect

The average amount of time it takes to collect your accounts receivables.

Salaries

The amount you are paying your team members in specific roles.

Cost of Customer Acquisition

Amount of expenses in marketing to acquire one customer.

Formula: Marketing Expenses / Number of Customers Acquired

How Do I Increase My Profit?

Now that you have gone through all of your numbers and even created new numbers to help, we can look at balancing your sales mix and examining ways to plus-up your current offer.

First, look at what percentage is coming from high-profit margin versus low-profit margin sales.

Now, take a look at how much you are spending on high-profit margin sales versus low-profit margin sales. This comparison will help you gauge how you can better spend your money and create a game plan for how you are going to inject more high-profit margin sales into your mix. Allocating money for specific items in proportion to your overall budget will give insight into where to spend your capital to gain best outcomes.

Getting your mix right can include branching out into bringing more product lines together. You need to be careful, though, that you are not spending too much of your budget on betting whether a new product will take off with your customers. Identifying great add-on sale items that come with high-profit margins is the key to bolstering your overall profit margin. Don't be scared to try something new but make sure you educate your team on the benefits of selling the new products. If you have their support and they are educated, you are increasing your new products' potential success.

It's always easier to sell to existing customers than to find new ones. Getting feedback from your customers on what they would like to get from your business is always helpful for making more informed decisions. You can achieve that feedback in many different ways from just straight out asking the right questions to giving out surveys. You will most likely get opinions from the happiest or unhappiest people, so you will need to set up the survey to give you an average response. A very crucial part of the business plan would be the break-even analysis as well as the profit forecast. These two calculations will give you an insight into how you must run your business in the first few months of operations and give comfort to financers as to your ability to repay the debt. While we are on that subject, don't try to convince a financer to loan you money on a truck that is in poor condition. Either find something new or in excellent condition or get a quote to put the truck in top condition. Do not expect a bank or finance company to lend its money on a bad truck and don't even think about doing that yourself. This is not a place to shortcut.

Let's take a look at how to compute for the break-even points first.

BEP or break-even point, in the context of a food truck operation, should be thought of in terms of:
P which symbolizes the price of each dish;
X which symbolizes the number of units per dish served.
V which symbolizes the variable cost per unit. Variable costs consist of costs that contribute directly to the forming of each unit of products (e.g. ingredients to make the food, gas used for cooking). Variable costs are not standard and vary depending on the usage.
FC symbolizes the fixed costs that are incurred per month. Fixed costs are standard costs that you have to pay whether or not you make any money or not (e.g. electricity bill, phone bill, web server costs).

Now that we have the variables defined, let's talk about how to use them in a formula to solve for break-even points.

First, you can look for the BEP in units so you know how much food you should sell to reach the break-even point for the first year of operations. The BEP in units can be solved like this:

BEP X = FC/V-P

This is X (number of units to BEP) is equal to FC (fixed costs) divided by V (variable costs) minus P (unit price per dish).

Once you have the BEP number of units, you can now determine your BEP price. You simply multiply the price per unit and the BEP number of units to get your BEP price.

It is formulated as follows:

BEP Price = X (BEP X)

Now, this formulation is just assuming that you have one product in your store. However, since you have a food truck, you will most likely have a lot of dishes on your menu (including drinks and add-ons).

With this in mind, the more appropriate formulation to use would be to get the weighted averages for selling price and variable costs. After you get these two, you can plot them into your formula.

To get the weighted average, you can use this formula:

(Selling price of product 1 × Sales percentage of product 1) + (Selling price of product 2 × Sales percentage of product 2) + (Selling price of product 3 × Sales percentage of product 3) + (Selling price of product 4 × Sales percentage of product 4)........

To get the Sales percentage of the product, you have to decide on a ranking of the products to determine which will sell the most to which would sell the least. The total percentage of all the products will equal 100%, so you have to split the 100% to all these products.

Once you've computed the weighted average of all your dishes, then you also compute the weighted average for variable costs as shown below:

(Variable expenses of product 1 × Sales percentage of product 1) + (Variable expenses of product 2 × Variable expenses of product 2) + (Variable expenses of product 3 × Sales percentage of product 3) + (Variable expenses of product 4 × Sales percentage of product 4) ....

After getting your weighted averages for variable costs and the selling prices, you can plot them into this formula:

BEP X = FC/ Weighted Average V - Weighted Average P

To better understand how to do this, we'll make use of a case scenario as an example.

Let's say you want to open up a burger food truck called Billy's Burger Stop wherein you will sell different kinds of burgers along with some fries and drinks.

At the start of the business, Billy's wants to introduce 3 burgers, 1 kind of fries, and lemonade.

Billy's will be selling Angus Burgers at $8,

Veggie Burgers at $7,

and Bacon Burgers at $8.

Billy's would also be selling fries at $4

And lemonade at $2.

Variable expenses would include $3 for Angus Burger,

$2.5 for Veggie Burgers,

$3 for Bacon Burgers,

fries at $1.50

and lemonade at 50c.

Billy's decided that the Angus Burger will have an SPP (sales percentage of product) of 30%,

Veggie Burgers 20%,

Bacon Burgers 20%,

fries at 10%

and lemonade at 20%.

To compute for the Break-even point, first, we compute for the weighted average of the selling price.

This would be (8x30%) + (7x20%) + (8x20%) + (4x10%) + (2x20%) = 5.6

After that, you get the weighted average of the variable cost which would be:

(3x30%) + (2.5x20%) + (3x20%) + (1.5x10%) + (0.5x20%) = 2.25

From there, we can plot the figures into the formula. Let's pack the FC at around $4,000 for everything including kitchen expenses, gas, rental, etc.

This will be 4,000/5.6-2.25 = 1045 units. This means that your truck would have to sell approximately 1,045 units to break-even.

Creating the Profit Forecast

After you know how to compute for the Break-even Point, you can now go ahead and make your profit forecast. Your profit forecast is very important because it will help you determine what month you can reach break-even and when you will start profiting. You will also see all of your expenses to know how to do some pencil-pushing. Let's get started with the expenses.

Compiling All Expenses

Before you create the profit forecast, you must first list down all of your expenses. When you start your food truck business, you must think first about your overhead expenses which are the expenses that you use to get the business going. These would include the cost to get the truck, the advertising wrap for the truck, and the food inventory for the first six months. We have included a food cost projection tool, that allows for accurate planning on a per dish basis.

For your truck, you may choose to either rent or buy one. If you are renting a food truck, you will be paying a monthly fee for the usage while if you buy one, you will just pay everything outright, unless you get a note on the vehicle.

Be sure to think about what would be the kitchen expenses, particularly extra equipment that must be purchased or rent if using a prep kitchen.

You must also think about designing your truck and your truck advertising. Aside from that, you should also take into consideration the labor that you will use for your truck. Assistants and cooks may be needed depending on how big you want your business to be at the start.
If you plan to start lean, you may just have 2 or 3 prep and cooking staff.

Lastly, you must source for your ingredients and add that as expenses. These are the major expenses you have to think of.

Monthly Expense Forecasting Tool

	Month 1		
	Price	**Quantity**	**Total Sales in Dollars**
Unit Price	xxx	xxx	$ xxx
Less: Cost of Sales	xxx	xxx	xxx
Profit per Piece	xxx		xxx
Security Deposit and Advanced Rental Expense			xxx
Truck Purchase/Rent			xxx
Kitchen Purchase/Rent			xxx
Marketing Expenses			xxx
Business License and Registration			xxx
Utility Expenses			xxx
Salaries Expenses			xxx
Truck Design Expense			xxx
Miscellaneous Expense			xxx
Insurance			xxx
Total Expenses			XXX
Net Income/Loss			xxx

This forecasting table was designed to project costs on a per month basis.

It contains the price, the quantity, and the total price in dollars. The price heading would determine the unit price and the quantity heading would determine the estimated quantity that you can sell in the first month. The unit price multiplied by the estimated quantity will equal total sales in dollars.
You will also have the unit price row heading along with the cost of sales. To get the profit per piece, you have to subtract the cost of sales from the unit price. Under the total sales in dollars column heading, you will get the total gross profit for the month.

Right below that is the list of expenses. The list of expenses is to be totaled in order to get the total expenses for the month. From there we subtract the total expenses from the gross profit and we get the net income/net loss for the month. If the total profit exceeds total expenses, we have a net income, if it doesn't, then we have a net loss.

It is also through this table that you can determine how long it will take for you to reach your break-even point. Take note that this tool doesn't assume any additional or prior capital infusion.

Determining Capital Requirement

By determining the income forecast, you now can determine the required capital infusion for the business. Most people are conservative and would infuse capital to cover the first three to six months of expenses whether or not the business reaches the break-even point and count on the sales to increase. This gives you a window to make mistakes, learn what your real sales are and what items on your menu are driving business. It certainly makes sense to revisit financial projections, break-even, and profit/loss analysis every 30 days or so, in the beginning, to avoid purchasing food that you won't use or incurring unnecessary expenses.

Complete the projection tool above and plan for the number of months you will cover regardless of sales and base your capital requirement on the number reached by computing the total expenses for a period of time plus the cost of sales for the said period of time.

If you are borrowing capital to start the business, consider negotiating a delay in the first payment on the note for 90-120 days to allow you to reinvest in the business, so there is sufficient capital in the business for operations.

Accept Credit Cards Anywhere

If you run a food truck business or are in the process of getting it up and running, you are going to need to establish a way to accept payments from your customers. When the food truck industry was just starting to gain momentum, there weren't a lot of choices to choose from. Food truck owners mainly had to accept cash or checks and maybe use the old carbon paper-based credit card imprint machines. When you only accept cash, you limit the number of customers that can purchase from your truck.

Outside of the food truck industry, it's amazing that some restaurants still only accept cash! These days, not a lot of people carry around cash with them... and if they do, it's usually just a small amount. Most customers expect a business to be able to accept credit or debit card purchases. Imagine yourself in that same situation when you've ordered food or tried to buy something from a merchant that only accepted cash, only to find you had no cash on you. How would you feel when you are told that the transaction is cash only?

That is exactly how your customers will feel if they are not given the choice to use their credit card. But thanks to innovative entrepreneurs and their technology; mobile payment apps and portable card readers are now available for any type of business. You can now accept almost any type of credit card on the go. These mobile Point-of-Sale systems or POS are the cornerstone of how payments are made in the food truck industry today. If you have a smartphone or tablet, you can get up and running very quickly.

Mobile is all the rage when it comes to food trucks and how they process credit card transactions. The mobile solutions available on the market today provide new opportunities for new and existing food truck businesses. With the success of the current systems available, it's inevitable that more competitors will off their mobile payment solutions in the future. But no matter how many competitors enter the marketplace, you need to understand the basics of how all credit card systems work.

With so many choices on the market, choosing a mobile credit card payment system for your food truck business can be difficult. How do you make the right choice when they all have similar features and functionality? Do you make a decision based on the lowest fees or maybe the best customer feedback and reviews?

This book was not written to decide for you but rather to give you informative insight into the features, functionality, and details of mobile payment systems in general. This book also highlights the most popular units on the market so you can compare the features and operating procedures associated with each company. I want you to have the information you need to help you make the best choice for your business needs.

Every food truck business is different and each team has different dynamics when it comes to operations. Your expenses and expected volume of sales can play into which mobile payment system integrates into your business the best. No payment system is perfect and you probably won't find one with every feature you want.

CHAPTER 5:

Expenses and Cash Flow

Starting a business is expensive and you need to know how to cover your start-up costs before you can get your food truck idea off the drawing board and onto the streets. There's no doubt that menu planning and designing your truck are considered the "fun" aspects of this business. While it can also be fun running a food truck, just remember that it is still a business and should be treated like one. Looks can be deceiving but starting a food truck business is just like starting a regular restaurant except for the mobility and lower start-up costs. It's not a get rich quick business! It takes long hours and dedication to make it and survive in this industry.

To be successful, you need to watch your cash flow. This is achieved through proper pricing and smart supply purchases. Also, you need to keep a close eye on expenses. There are no set costs for starting a gourmet food truck business. Each food truck is unique and has different requirements. Start by making a list of all the expenses you can think of. Don't be surprised if your costs add up fast. You will need to calculate how much it costs to produce each dish. This is important because, in the beginning, you need to get a good idea of the amount of money needed to start and maintain your business. And don't forget legal, accounting, and other financial expenses.

Operating Expenses

Another part of the equation is operating expenses. Operating expenses are the ongoing costs that keep your business running. You can consider operating costs like recurring monthly payments. Breaking it down even further gives us fixed and variable expenses. Examples of fixed expenses can include commissaries, vehicle payments, vehicle rental, website hosting, and insurance. When it comes to variable expenses, ingredients, fuel, repairs, marketing, and special permits can fall into this category. It's important to be able to estimate your costs each month as accurately as possible. And you might need to anticipate a little extra for the unknown. Unexpected costs can come from last-minute events or vehicle repairs.

Keep in mind that it's going to take time for your business to become profitable. And it can be hard to watch the money fly out the door without any return on investment in the early months. The bigger your initial investment, the longer it will take to pay it back. One advantage of a food truck is that it has lower overhead costs. However, you will still need enough capital on-hand to be able to continue running for at least six months to a year in the beginning. Studies have shown that it often takes businesses at least two years to start showing profits. For most people, that is an eternity!

Managing Food Volume

You will need to effectively manage the volume of food. Here are the variables that help determine volume. Part of it is how much food you will buy and how much of it you are going to prepare. Then you will need to figure out how much you are going to sell. Calculating volume can be difficult. You can estimate your volume in the beginning to get a ballpark figure but only experience will make you better at estimating how much to buy and prepare.

The ongoing dilemma is figuring out how much food to bring to a service. This depends on how much you think you can sell. Often you won't know until you run out of food. And when you do run out of food, you won't know how much food you could've sold! This can be very frustrating.

The other challenge is that you only have a limited time to sell your food because you are not open all day like a traditional restaurant. You need to be able to serve foods quickly and increase volume. Another aspect that comes into play is pricing your menu correctly. There needs to be a balance in your pricing. If your prices are too high you won't sell much food. If your prices are too low, you won't make any money. On average, most food truck items are priced between $6 to $10 but some charge more.

Building Loyal Customers

To build a strong following for your truck, you need to have affordable prices. You can compare the prices of similar items from your competitors. Charging the right price is another skill that comes from experience. Your location plays a factor in determining what your customers will want to pay. Pricing in one city will be different than that in another city. Portion size helps determine your price also.

You need to identify what makes your food different from the competition. If you charge much higher than the competition, then you need to justify why it costs more.

Here are some reasons that you can charge more for your food than your competitors. You might be using organic ingredients or maybe you are including side dishes not offered by your competitors. Your portion size may be larger. Maybe you are using imported ingredients. Serving a gluten-free menu can also justify a higher price. The bottom line here is that if you are spending more than you are making, then adjustments will have to be made.

Adjustments you can make are lowering supply costs, getting bulk discounts for your ingredients, adjustments to employees, and staff size, you could join a co-op or you can improve your marketing strategies. When you've calculated your costs, determine how many items you need to sell just to break even.

The first year is going to be the most difficult to become profitable! The first year is also where most adjustments will be made. And of course, there'll be some factors that are out of your control like:

- Bad weather

- Event cancellations

- Health issues

- Vehicle breakdowns

It's all part of the business and every industry is faced with the same hurdles. Having lots of patience can go a long way to get you through the toughest parts of the start-up process.

CHAPTER 6:

Marketing Strategies and Prices, Promotions, etc.

Offer Something for Free

Offering something small for free to each customer is a good way to ensure happy customers and to distinguish you from other trucks. It is also good for keeping people occupied. As the orders come piling in and the wait time becomes longer, giving people something small to snack on is a good way to keep them occupied until their food arrives. People can become impatient with the longer wait times but if they've already received something, they'll be more patient with you.

It all depends on what type of food you like to make but it is easy to give out free items that don't cost much. We've done homemade popcorn and homemade chips, as well as small desserts.

A small bag of popcorn to each person waiting won't cost you much and the benefits will be a happier and more tolerant customer. I have found this to be a good way to get a more friendly and loyal customer base, especially if you continually serve at a particular location.

Let the Order Line Be Longer Than the Pickup Line

This may sound a bit confusing so let me explain. If you have a large number of people waiting to order as well as people waiting for their food, it's a better idea to make the people looking to order wait than it is to let the people looking to pick up wait.

Once people have ordered, they're ready to take it and go; they get impatient very quickly. They know their order has been received and they're not thinking about all the other orders on the board, they just want theirs. People waiting to order, on the other hand, are only impatient because there are people in front of them in-line and so their impatience lies more with the people ahead of them than it does with you.

With a long list of orders on the board, things will get stressful in the truck pretty quickly. You will want to take orders but also be scrambling to get food orders out the window. However, from experience, it's better to hold off on taking more orders if there's a large number already on the board to concentrate on.

Let the people waiting to order know that you are busy clearing the board and will be with them shortly and focus on getting some of the orders out to waiting customers. That way you will keep people's wait times for their food down, which is generally more important than the line waiting to order.

Offer Items from Your Catering Menu

Though this book doesn't focus on the catering side of your business, serving food on the street is a good chance to promote it. A good way to do this is to offer 1 or 2 items from your catering menu. Assuming you have a catering menu, a good way to land catering gigs is to choose a couple of items from this menu for street service.

Now maybe your catering food is more tailored towards cocktail parties and smaller foods but that's fine. You can offer them as a side, give some out for free or change the item to make it more of a main dish and less of a smaller finger food type.

However, you do it, it's good to test out how people like the items you will be serving at your catering events. It will also be a good chance for people who may be planning a catering gig to get a taste of what they can expect if they book their gig with you.

If you make sure to promote it and make a note on your menu that the item is from your catering menu, it will let people know that you do cater and that this is the quality they can expect. So besides satisfying people's taste buds on the street, you will be subtly promoting your catering, which is where you can make very good money.

Assuming your food tastes great, this is a good way to attract people to your catering business and give people the idea of booking their gig with you.

Always Ask If They Would Like A Drink

This may sound painfully obvious but it's easy to forget. Especially if you are busy, you will be too focused on taking orders and getting food out the window and you may forget to ask each customer if they'd like a drink. In addition to putting drinks on the menu, it's a good idea to ask each person if they'd like to add a drink if they haven't already asked for one.

Every dollar counts and this is a good and effortless way to make a couple of extra bucks out of each order, which throughout a day of selling will start to add up. Again, you will want to price your food so that adding a drink can add to a number that goes with a bill. This won't be possible in all cases but try to keep it in mind.

For example, maybe your main item sells for $8. It isn't a stretch to ask 2 dollars for a can of Coke and most people won't think twice about handing you a 10-dollar bill. It's always a good idea as well to offer a discount if they include a drink with their meal or for a combo deal with a drink and a side.

Whatever you decide, be sure to ask every customer if they'd like to add a drink. A lot of people who wouldn't order one will end up getting one; you just have to put the idea in their head.

Advertise Your Menu on Social Media

This is important for several reasons. You will want your regular customers to know what you will be offering that day and hopefully, it's something they've had before and want to try again. It's also for people who haven't tried your truck. This is where a good menu is important, with great-sounding food. You will want those good descriptions to catch their eye and entice them to come and check your truck out.

I've found that it's rather boring just to write out what you are offering that day, especially if your main social media advertising is on hosts that are picture-based. This is where taking pictures of your food is important, as you can show them what you will be offering as well as describe it. This is where you will get people excited.

If they see what you are offering and it looks great, they'll be much more inclined to come to enjoy your food than if you were to just describe it. This can be done in many different posts, one for each item. That way you will give more people a chance to see your posts and they'll be able to see everything you are offering, hopefully enticing them to be excited about a number of your items.

In addition to pictures, add what each item consists of; just write the same description that's on your menu. The picture and description should be enough for people to want to come down and check it out. If your pictures look good and the description is intriguing, this shouldn't be difficult.

You should do this with your location: Throwing up a picture of what you will be serving and letting them know where and when they can enjoy it is a great way to combine these two. Do this when you know your location, throughout the week, and the day before and day of. That way you will build some anticipation and give more people a chance to see what they can hope to enjoy and how to get it.

Make Sure the Spot's Worth It

After spending all this time and money, you will want to make sure that, on average, you are making money. It's not as easy as it looks to turn a profit on a food truck. There are so many factors that are working against you, most of which you can't control. It may sound like I'm being negative but the truth is, losses can begin to pile up quickly and as such it's important from the get-go to recognize this and do what you can to mitigate these losses.

Whether it be bad weather, a poor customer turnout, or just pure bad luck, you will want to identify quickly if the spot you've chosen is worth it. Often, you will return to the same spot many weeks in a row. This makes sense, as it's not easy to find spots to park your truck, whether that's because of city regulations or because there just aren't that many good places to sell food. Whatever it is, you will want to decide quickly whether the spot you find yourself at is a spot you should continue to attend.

In a lot of instances, good spots can end up costing money before you even show up. This will depend on your city but sometimes your best bet is on private property and you will end up shelling over a reasonable amount of cash just for the right to sell there. This can be a minor expense if the spot is great but if it isn't, you could find yourself at a loss at the end of the day.

Factoring in the fee to be there, food costs, truck costs, not to mention all the hours you put into making the food, you want to be turning a profit and if you are not, odds are you should find a new spot. Often, to focus on all the other factors that go into running a food truck business is easy but finding a good location, which is a big part of making money, is forgotten.

Be honest with yourself and if the spot sucks, don't keep showing up. Save that money you'd otherwise be wasting and find somewhere new where you can hope to establish a good customer base. It's better to go back to the drawing board than to keep throwing money at a venture that isn't profitable, especially at the early stages when you can't afford to waste money.

Proximity to like vendors: When participating in festival events, ask the event organizer to not place you next to food vendors that sell the same entrée items you are selling. Meaning if BBQ Pulled Pork is on your menu and your neighboring food vendor is selling BBQ Pulled Pork you are in direct competition with them. This can lead to confusion among prospective patrons and dwindle your sales.

These Pizza Truck vendors are in direct competition with each other

Best location: As you plan to participate in various events, some food vendor applications will allow you to select where you prefer to setup. As a general rule of thumb always select spots near the Beer Garden, Bathrooms, and ATMs. Why? Two words...**Foot Traffic**.

- Foot Traffic is your best friend when participating in festival events. Being close to the Beer Garden, Bathrooms and ATMs provide prospective vendors with the greatest exposure to patrons attending festival events.

Electrical power and water: The essentials of operating your food truck at festival events are water and electrical power. Electricity is required to operate your refrigeration equipment and water is required to wash your hands and dishes. Keep the following things in your hip pocket as you prepare:

- Bring an extension cord long enough to reach the power supply receptacle, a 50ft cord is sufficient.

- If you are unable to have a direct water connection from the event water source, bring a 5-gallon water jug to refill your freshwater tanks.

- Know how to reset the electrical breaker in case the power source gets overloaded with multiple electrical connections from other vendors.

Note the three hoses connected to the water spigot, two connections are directly connected to a food truck vendor's water source, the single-detached hose is for refilling water buckets.

Include a portable non-potable water container for collecting wastewater and a potable water container for clean water in your equipment inventory.

- Not all electrical and water source connections are the same, be prepared with various electrical adapters and water hoses in case the event organizer is unable to accommodate your connection needs.

Generator "Don't be that guy": There may be times when electricity is not available at the festival event due to logistics and the use of a generator is required. As a courtesy, always position your generator at least 25 feet away and behind your food truck or trailer. Generators produce a lot of noise. The noise produced by generators will disrupt customer interaction and make it difficult to hear patrons place their orders.

- Don't be that rude food vendor with a loud generator that disrupts fellow food vendors taking orders from customers.

Amperage; know what your equipment pulls: When filling in food vendor applications you will note a section reserved for amperage requirements. Typically, 20 AMPS or 30 AMPS is the norm. This is assessed by adding the total amperage of the electrical output of equipment installed on your food truck or trailer. Look at the specification label of your equipment to determine the amperage. When you identify the amperage for each electrical item used, the collective sum will be the total amperage you will include on your vendor application.

Finally, understand the appropriate electrical cords capable of carrying the correct electrical load for your food truck or trailer. Most food trucks operate on a 220 Volt 4-Prong connection and most food trailers operate on a 120 Volt 3-Prong connection.

Examples of various power plugs.

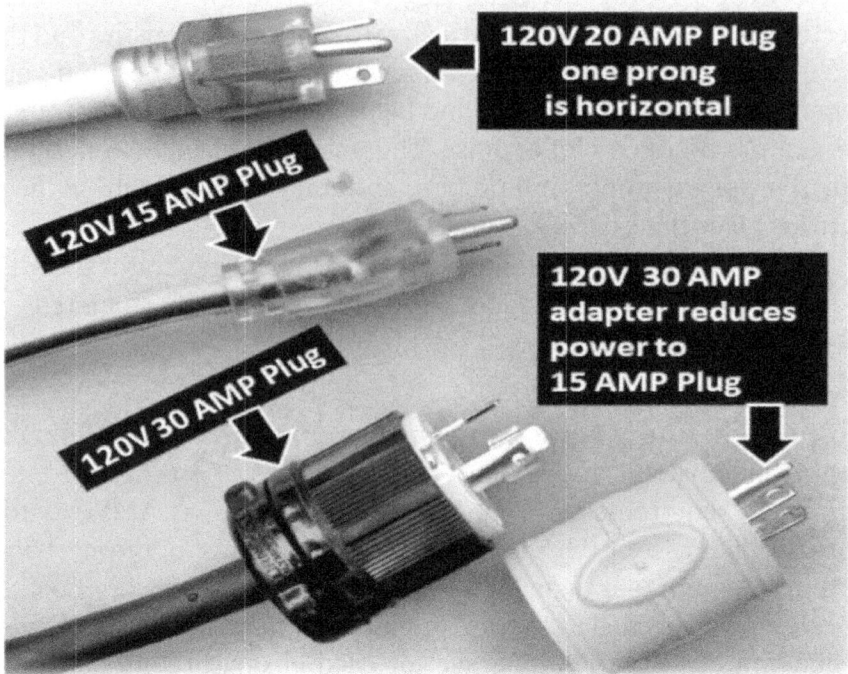

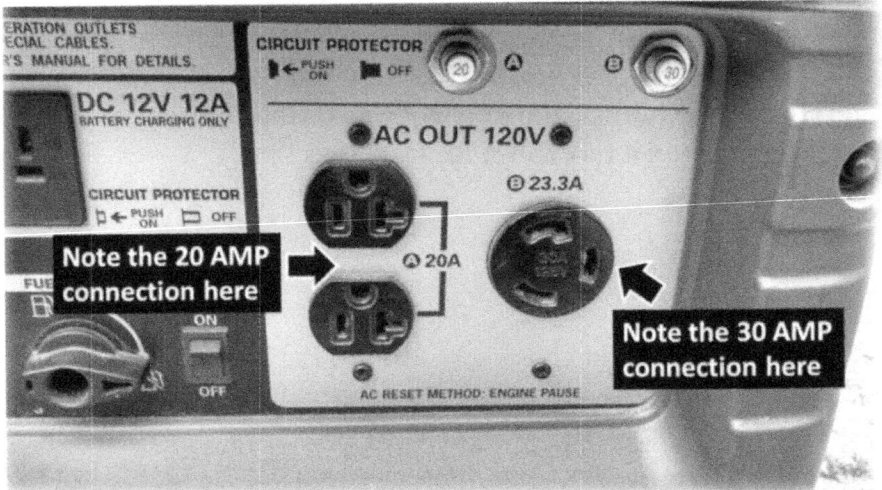

Electrical input connections for a Honda Generator

Food Truck Parking During Business Hours

Since space in larger cities is at such a premium, the rules for using said space are typically regulated more rigidly than they would be in a less populated city.

After you've scouted your food truck's prime spot, make sure you check with all local authorities what kind of permits and licenses you need to operate but also what's needed to keep it parked. Needs a special lease for space? What are the terms and conditions of the contract and are they transferable?

Food Truck Parking During Off Hours

When you've closed up the truck for the day, where are you parking it? When you live in the suburbs, you may have your driveway, where you can park the nighttime food truck. That's perfect because you don't have any additional costs. If you are not so lucky, you may need to hire or rent a space during non-business hours to park your food truck and that may add up to a few hundred dollars a month.

Event Parking

We will park this one right here because activities involving food trucks would normally cost you some money. Finding a prime location for your daily operations is critical to your restaurant's success on wheels but so is your involvement in food truck events— or events that feature a food truck aspect such as the Belmont Stakes Racing Festival Food Truck Village. Your attendance at these kinds of activities would typically cost only $200-$1000 to participate and the organizers may like a portion of your profits as well. Before committing, ensure you read the fine print.

Tools of Trade: Web Site, Cards, Stationery

So Much Digital Media, So Little Time

Once you have your first few events under your belt, it's time to make your business truly professional. You could have business cards and stationery made up before your first event but as I have suggested over and over, you are likely to change some things about your stand after you start doing events.

Preprinted stationery is so last century. Much more common now is to use a template in a word processing application for your letterhead. Business cards are incredibly easy to design and have printed these days.

A web site is another matter. To my way of thinking, every business ought to have a web site. I've been told my way of thinking is biased because I'm a "computer guy." That may be true and I enjoy designing my web pages, posting photos and videos from events to my "Pictures" pages, and maintaining an online calendar of my event bookings. But even if you have no computer skills at all, having a website for your business is incredibly easy.

You don't need any of the advanced code-writing used by sites with online ordering, logins, databases, or java script. A vendor web page only needs a few pictures and text. Your nineteen-year-old niece or nephew could probably do it for you. Your website should have a brief description of your business, a menu, or product guide, and how to contact you. This could all be on one page. For the more ambitious, the site could include a calendar page, pictures page, travel blog, cooking or crafting tips, or any other fun topic you might want to share.

The cost of having your own web site has dropped amazingly over the years. In the early days of the Internet, web site hosting and domain name registration could cost hundreds of dollars a month. Now those services can be found for under ten bucks a month. There are even services that will host your site free. The drawback is, since they have to make their money somehow, no-charge hosts will use your site's pages to post advertising banners.

Once your business is established, your website could become another source of revenue. This is especially true for merchandise vendors. Adding order forms, shopping carts and online payment options makes a website more complicated to design but imagine how nice it would be to increase your sales by a few hundred bucks a month from people ordering your products on the web.

Food vendors can develop supplemental catering businesses. What a great way to maintain an income during the offseason. A web site is vital for supporting and promoting a separate catering venture.

The next section is on social media, where I will state emphatically and repeatedly that you do not need to devote hours of your life to social media. However, you do need some kind of web presence. Having no Internet involvement at all these days is like not having an e-mail address or phone number. If a website seems more trouble than you care to take on, at least put up a Facebook page. Your business will not be perceived as legitimate if no one can find you on the Internet.

Social Media

Ugh, how to tackle this one. Just hearing about social media gives me the creeps. We're bombarded with reports about Facebook trends, what's happening in the "Twittersphere," who's hot on Instagram. If you are into social media, use social media; if you are not, don't. Some people swear you MUST post regularly to all social media outlets. You have to tell all your followers what you are doing and where you are going to be all the time! Really? Do you think hundreds of Instagram followers are going to attend a festival, simply because a vendor posted a picture of their stand from the festival? Would people who aren't fans of country music attend a country music jamboree, just to visit a single vendor?

Sure, I get it, social media is fun—for folks who think social media is fun. Heck, I post pictures and videos from events to my website regularly. However, I don't expect people to come to events and visit my booth because of my website posts. My website is designed to impress event organizers and for the fun of letting friends and family see the crazy stuff, I get myself into.

If you've figured out a way to make social media marketing work for you and you like doing it, go crazy with it! If you aren't into devoting huge chunks of your life to tweeting, posting, commenting, and tagging, your business will grow fine without it.

Maintaining a social media presence is a part-time job. The five, ten, twenty hours a week you have to commit to posting updates could be much better spent on other elements of your business. That is unless you LIKE posting updates. If social media is your recreation, knock yourself out. But don't believe astonishing success will follow if you spend half your waking hours seeking followers. Every business does not have to tweet or fail. Not everyone likes social media.

Driving in a tunnel makes it hard to see other roads. People in the social media tunnel, tell us the only way to succeed is with social media. Meanwhile, only a tiny fraction of social media messages reaches the viewers. How many of the half-billion tweets posted yesterday did you read? If you could read one Tweet every five seconds and all you did was read Tweets all day every day, you would not live long enough to read all the Tweets posted yesterday. Don't get the jitters over Twitter. Likewise, don't fret over Facebook. How many of the 2.5 billion Facebook users do you follow or follow you?

Forgive me if my view on social media seems harsh. I don't despise using digital devices to connect with people and I don't scorn people who love tweeting and tagging and posting. I'm simply fed up with the worship of social media. We're told social media is the end-all, be-all marketing tool for all businesses and professions. That simply is not true.

Social media is wonderful—for people who think social media is wonderful. Those people can use it, live their lives on it, spend half their days on it, if that's what they're into. If you love social media, you will find ways to benefit from it. If you don't love social media, don't worry; your vending business will get along fine without it.

Mobile vending is what I call a "non-relationship" business. We don't need to chase social media followers. A customer buys something from us and goes on their way. We don't know their name; we don't create a record of their purchase history and we don't need to stay in touch with them after the sale.

After you've been in business for a few years and you've done the same events several times, you will be delighted when repeat customers begin to seek you out. I beam with pride when people see my stand and tell their friends, "Oh good, Tropic Hut is here again. You have to try their Java Silkie!"

That's very satisfying but proud as it may make me feel, I'm sure no one would attend a festival solely because my Tropic Hut stand was there. It's wonderful to see repeat customers. I don't need to have them follow me online.

Relationship businesses are things like banking, real estate, advertising, and insurance. People in those businesses are perpetually networking, going to business mixers, and Chamber of Commerce functions–and desperately pursuing social media followers. They're the ones who chase followers. Did you catch the irony of that? Chasing followers?

We mobile vendors may not form relationships with our customers but we are wise to build a network of fellow vendors and event organizers. After all, to get to our customers we have to get into events. Good relations with other vendors and event organizers get us into better events.

I send Christmas Cards to the organizers of events I work each year. Fellow vendors I've become friends with are also on my Christmas Card list, as well as in my e-mail address book. In this age of political correctness, some may not be into sending Christmas Cards. In that case, send non-religious New Year greeting cards: "Looking forward to another year of great fun and successful festivals!"

If I come across something interesting or funny, I share it with my vending buddies in a group e-mail. On several occasions, fellow vendors have tipped me off to good events or recommended me to event organizers. When organizers of good festivals start inviting you to participate in their events, that's when you know you've arrived.

Note that none of my social interactions with event organizers or fellow vendors is expected to gain customers for my vending business. It's networking with event organizers so I can gain access to customers at festivals and it's socializing with others in my field but it's not intended or expected to reach customers directly. If that's how you use social media—you know, to socialize—your expectations are in the right place.

With that suggestion on networking, we come to the close of this guide. I hope you have found a few tips that help build a successful vending business. People sometimes ask what I think are the most important factors for a mobile vendor's success. I can narrow that down to three things: products, signage, and capacity to handle rushes.

CHAPTER 7:

Launching and Post-Launching Tips to Keep the Food Truck Running

The launchpad is ready to release and it is time to rev up the engines and stoves of the food truck. Marketing is essential to keep any business running. You should help the business to get noticed so that you can lure in customers. Competitors in the same field of business are never going to rest and make it easier for you. You must advertise and market yourself and your food product efficiently. Here are some marketing tips for the food truck business:

Set up weekly specials: After the launch, you must gain speed and traffic in business. If a customer likes a specific food item like a Mexican taco, you could have "Taco Tuesdays" where you serve the customers tacos at half the normal price. This will spread the word and will assure you a lot of crowds.

Be one with the community: Get close with the community you want to serve. Sponsor for a local sports event or try helping in a charity. Also, find ways to tie up with other business owners in the community.

Hold contests: People love contests and they are an excellent idea to promote your food truck business. Promote contests through social media and other forms of advertising.

Celebrate often: You do not need a big reason to celebrate. Opt for smaller holidays and make things exciting and new for the customers. Show the spirit of your celebration through the food you offer.

Have an inner circle: Treat your most valuable customers nicely and create an inner circle with them. Offer them discounts and earn their trust by being sweet and nice to them.

After all this, it is also important that you choose the perfect spot to put up the food truck. Make sure that you choose a place where there will be a lot of hungry people. Park your vehicle next to a commercial or industrial space. Also, make sure that there are no serious competitors around to spoil your day. When you want to choose a place, also find out about the events that might happen regularly at that place. Try to participate in such events and maximize your profit in doing so. Assure that you find out about the ease with which you can get the licenses to put up your food truck in these events. Do not feel bad to partner up. Partner up with a mall or building complex that will allow you to set up a spot on their property.

Tips to Sustain the Successful Run After Setting Up

It is essential to keep the business running in a smooth and controlled manner. This will make your brand profitable in the long run.

Feel free to market yourself

Marketing extends beyond the beginning phase and it is essential to keep the food truck running. Take advantage of digital media and its marketing platforms. Tweet about the places you are going to put up the stall, connect with Facebook, and maintain a Facebook page to post regular updates. Have a well-planned social media marketing scheme and try to lure in more customers by showing the merrier sides in dining with you. Also, make sure that you deliver the quality and service that you have advertised. False advertising can put a hole in the whole process.

Think freely and do not attach yourself to an idea

Even if you have found the perfect spot for business and even it had worked well for a long time, there is a possibility of dwindling of sales. Take time to re-plan and think about moving to another new area. Do not be too rigid in the way you think. It is a waste of time and you might end up losing the business in the process.

Expand on the revenue streams

Change over the course of time and try implementing new business ideas. Take risks and always be on the lookout for new opportunities. Cater to events and festivals to increase the profits you take. Get out of the comfort zone and try new and exciting things. Keep the energy and flow running.

Be open to teaming up

Do not feel bad about teaming up with other food truck owners out there. You could get a lot out of it because people who eat out of food trucks are most likely to change their trucks often. Pick a crowded place and a friendly food truck owner to club your business with. Cater to that crowded place together and get the best out of that situation. It need not be regularly but it is good to team up once in a while. People will also love the variety that you and your friend in business have to offer.

Keep networking

Make friends with people who have a strong influence over the place. Drop the prejudice and consider asking other truck owners to get valuable referrals for events and festivals. People might help you and you might even expand your network. Do not live in your world and miss out on the exposure that others have to offer to you.

Make a good investment in your staff

Make sure that you help the staff grow within their positions so that they stay trustworthy and faithful in the future. You must treat them with the respect they deserve and you must acknowledge their good work. The process of bringing in and training new staff is not only time-consuming but also costly.

Put a good price tag on your food items

Being new to the business doesn't mean that you have to offer food for a very cheap rate. If your food is tasty and has very good quality, feel free to charge the price that will benefit your system. It is vital to remember that people are ready to pay for the good stuff. Keep your eyes on the quality of the food you serve and you will automatically see a growth in business.

These tips and techniques are essential in your path to become a successful food truck owner. So, get out there and put out some interesting items on the menu to keep the hungry taste buds on fire. Serve with a bright smile on your face and complete love in your heart. There are a whole lot of people to feed in this world and it is high time that you realize that you can be the change you want to see. Thrive and work hard to serve the tastiest food on wheels and make sure that you touch the lives of people with what you do.

Food Safety

Food safety is a global issue, spanning several specific urban areas.

The food safety guidelines aim to prevent contamination of foods and that may cause food poisoning. It is done across various channels, some of which are:

- Sanitizing and proper cleaning of all surfaces, utensils, and equipment

- Maintaining a high standard of personal hygiene, in particular, handwashing

- Chilling, heating and storing food correctly with regards to equipment, environment, and temperature

- Introducing effective methods of pest control

- Understanding food poisoning, food intolerance, and food allergies

Regardless of the reason you are handling food, whether it's part of your profession or cooking at home, it's important to always follow the proper food health principles. There is any number of possible food hazards in a food handling environment, many of which have severe implications with them.

According to the new annual study by OzFoodNet, Tracking the Instances and Causes of Diseases Potentially Transmitted by Food in Australia, 5.4 million cases of foodborne disease occur in Australia per year which are preventable. The incidents caused by these diseases is estimated at an astounding AUD 1.2 billion.

In American food businesses when referring to food safety, ownership is placed solely on the business itself. It must ensure that all foods handled and prepared within the business are safe to eat. Many are expected to hire a qualified Food Safety Manager to help the food business fulfill this duty.

How to Get Smart About Food Safety?

If you have never worked in the food service industry you need to enroll in a program that certifies you and your employees with the necessary credentials that demonstrate your knowledge of food safety. ServSafe is the nationally recognized food code authority for the United States. They offer food safety training for food handlers and food managers that work in the restaurant industry. Many states are now requiring food service professionals to be ServSafe certified. Check with your local health department to see if this is a requirement for you.

Food Safety Resources

There are many food safeties resources out there to help educate you about proper food storage, food preparation, and food holding requirements. The bottom line is you need to be armed with the necessary information to protect the public from foodborne illnesses. Each state has different requirements but all state and city health departments develop their regulatory requirements based on the U.S. Food and Drug Administration's (FDA) Food Code. States and city health departments are permitted to add additional safety measures to their regulatory requirements to address additional safety concerns.

Here is a list of some public website resources to bookmark for future reference:

- U.S. Food and Drug Administration Public Website www.fda.gov - type in the keywords 'Food Code' on their search tool for the most current Food Code

- U.S. Department of Agriculture Public Website www.fsis.usda.gov - type in the keywords 'Food Safety Education' on their search tool for various insightful training on food safety.

- Nebraska Department of Agriculture Public Website www.nda.nebraska.gov - type in the keywords 'Focus on Food Safety' for an excellent guide on food safety

Why Must I Use Commercial Equipment?

The most common complaint I hear from new food truck operators and restaurateurs that have never worked in the food industry is "why do I have to purchase expensive commercial food equipment when the food equipment I use at home is just as good?" These aspiring entrepreneurs believe household refrigerators and freezers are sufficient to handle the day-to-day job required to operate their food establishment, not to mention household units are less expensive than commercial units.

Here is the answer to the aforementioned question: **the temperature recovery rate for refrigeration units designated for household use cannot keep up with the constant open and closing of the refrigeration doors during food truck or restaurant use.** Temperatures inside the cooling section of units for household use may exceed the safe temperature range for the food being held, resulting in bacteria growth and food safety risks passed on to the customer as foodborne illnesses.

If one of your customers gets sick due to you or your employees' failure to adhere to proper food safety, your business is done – you will be asking your old employer for your job back because you neglected to apply simple food safety procedures.

Commercial refrigeration units are not cheap and range from $1,200-$9,000 depending on the brand and the number of doors the unit is equipped with. Reach-in coolers need to be capable of keeping refrigerated foods at a temperature of 41°F or less. Reach-in freezers need to be capable of keeping frozen foods at a temperature of 0°F or less.

All commercial equipment used for the refrigeration, cooking, and or hot-holding of food will have a commercial-grade specification affixed to the unit. The most recognized commercial-grade standard is ANSI or NSF but some other standards also exist and are acceptable too. The bottom line, if your equipment is labeled "Household Use" it is not approved for commercial food service.

Some Basics About Food Safety

This part of your business is not the most glamorous part of your operation but trust me it will put you out of business if you do not take it seriously. Food safety does not require an advanced degree in Biology, just simple attention to detail. After you successfully pass the required food safety course requirements for the state where your business will operate keep a copy of the 'Focus on Food Safety' booklet, previously mentioned in the list of public website resources, on your food truck and review it with your employees monthly.

Maintaining Your Food Truck in The Winter

Half of the nation is encountering freezing cool, harsh climate during this part of the year. This is particularly noteworthy for organizations that partially or entirely rely upon climate conditions for deals. What's more, regardless of whether these businesses can discover approaches to keep deals up while they persevere through the chilly weather, they additionally need to keep up the working hardware that spends long periods of time outside.

Food trucks are no special case for this standard. Just like with vehicles, truck proprietors continually run into challenges with firing up the engine in cold conditions. Even though you and other catering truck proprietors should expect to set up your trucks before the winter season begins, if you haven't there are still simple approaches to do maintenance jobs and safety checks that are explicit to chilled air and winter driving before the end of the season. Here are a couple of steps to guaranteeing that your mobile food stand endures through the rest of the season:

Ensure your normal upkeep is up to date

If you do this during the snowy season, you can help ensure that you don't experience unforeseen repairs.

Take a look at your antifreeze

To help protect your food vehicle, ensure that your truck contains a full degree of 50/50 blend of antifreeze and water all through the season. You can get this investigated at a service station or test it yourself with the proper device.

Check your tires

Winter isn't a simple season on your tires. On a cold highway, these are the most significant highlights among you and the guard rails. The National Highway Transportation Safety Board reports that you need at least 2/32" of profundity to be protected. What's more, check your tire strain to ensure that your altogether siphoned up-tires will, in general, not lose pressure in the cold.

Review and replace your wipers

Your wipers are even progressively susceptible to damage when you and your food trailer's group are continually utilizing them to remove ice, debris, snow, and hail from the windshield. When you are driving, you rely upon your wipers to clear anything from your vision that is laying on the exterior, so it's basic to ensure they can carry out their responsibility. In the winter it turns out to be considerably progressively essential to focus on your catering food truck's wipers as your truck will encounter sand and salt from the highway department's snow cleanup schedule.

Watch out for your windshield washer liquid

It's a tendency for vehicle proprietors to utilize an abundance of washer liquid to help melt ice from the windshield of their food trucks' in the winter. As this is the situation, ensure that you check and replace your washer liquid.

Proceed with your yearly upkeep as necessary, in addition to your winter maintenance

So, as to ensure that your food trailer is performing well all year, you should normally clean your battery posts, examine your spark plug wires, investigate your brakes and check your motor oil.

Complete these undertakings throughout the winter season so, your food truck and its passengers can be as prepared and safe in the cold weather as possible. Try not to let this season put you out of commission!

Successful Food Truck Marketing

Food truck occasions!

A food truck occasion displays an extraordinary chance to attract the interest of both new and existing purchasers. These occasions are regularly composed by somebody attempting to make a buck on collecting rents to be a part of the occasion but that is life in America. It very well may be justified, despite all the trouble but you should verify who else will be there and who is the clientele attending. You certainly don't need competition in your food. Furthermore, you would prefer not to serve your vegan cooking to a lot of rodeo types. Similarly, as with anything, thoroughly consider the cooperative energy of attending and figure if the cost to do it merits the potential return.

Different sorts of occasions might be functions of associations that need to pull in individuals to their organization or events. These undertakings offer an enormous upside since you will be connected in the client's observation with the association supporting the occasion. That can give great PR.

A key factor to the accomplishment of an occasion relies upon the coordinator's investment into appropriate advertising of the occasion, to incorporate catchy posters and fliers. Some attention ought to be paid to your food truck and the role it plays in the bigger event. Try not to be shy to demand what inclusion you and your truck will have in this advertising.

Putting resources into your very own Branding.

Here you will have the test of putting inadequate time and center to branding something that if you have no experience with it will be difficult. I propose you go with an organization that offers branding and marketing services. Branding has a gigantic upside, for it separates you from your opposition memorably and uniquely, it's classy to have your own branded items.

Your name reveals everything...

Or possibly it should try to. A name is generally critical to pass on in a short and direct fashion as possible what you are, what you do, and in case of food, what you serve. What about Sizzle Stix (a Gourmet Street's brand) that sells tasty kabob foods skewered on a stick. Get it? What about Sweeties, they serve everything for the sweet tooth. What do you think the Dog Truck sells? (I'm not proposing this, you may get a young man who wants to purchase a dog from you). But you get my point, I hope. There's the "Take the Dump Truck." Can you think about what it sells? Dumplings... I don't think so!

Ensure your truck is appealing.

It's genuinely counterproductive to spend all the cash on a new, completely equipped food truck, just to leave it standard and dull. A lovely vinyl wrap, stupendously structured is definitely worth the cash and will attract the eye of all who you drive by. Get innovative and make an external appearance that matches the alluring food you are offering inside.

Train your staff to have astounding customer service.

It ought to be your #1 priority, as the initial five seconds of cooperation between another client and your staff will either make a client or the inverse, best case scenario, the customer may leave and pass-by disinterested and even under the least favorable conditions, cause somebody to insult your truck to other people. Train your staff to smile always, be selfless and benevolent.

Qualities That A Food Truck Vendor Must Have

In the past, individuals thought of food trucks as a source of junk food. Anyway, as time passed by, the value and the functionality of food trucks have been uncovered. Individuals who are swamped at work and have no opportunity to take their lunch in the solaces of their homes or eateries rely on food truck proprietors to bring them healthy meals.

In view of the notoriety of vending trucks, few people who might need to earn are venturing to this kind of business. If you wish to be a successful food truck trader, you should have the following attitudes:

Patience

Finding a vehicle that you can transform into a vending truck involves a great deal of time. There are a lot of organizations that sell vehicles that are perfect for being converted into food trucks. If you lack the patience in scouring the market for the best deal that you can get, at that point, you might be deceived by merchants who take advantage of the high demand for vehicles. If you need to set aside cash and get the best vehicle you should be able to look for the best deal.

Innovator

A food seller should be productive. Being innovative means being to get the same number of requests as you can from the workplaces that are situated at places where your food truck will pass on. If the seller is innovative, then he will be able to convey his products to numerous workplaces and offices.

Friendly

Significantly, you can assemble affinity with your clients. This is because if they consider you to be a well-known face and a business person who considers nothing but profits. Friendliness means you will be selling a greater amount of your merchandise and items.

Creative

Clients don't care for routine food. This is the reason why they would avoid heading off to the office cafeteria to eat their meals. You should be creative in your menus. Ensure that you have an assortment of food that you can offer to your clients. It won't just satisfy your clients; however, you will likewise be able to remain in front of your competition.

Time Management

Manage time successfully. You should recall that the basic reason why you are starting a food truck business is for adaptability and freedom rather than simply being positioned in one location. If you can manage your time well, then you can serve numerous clients. The more places you can visit in one day, the more clients you serve, the more profits you gain.

The food truck business is anything but a difficult business to learn. If you have every one of these attributes, then you will unquestionably become wildly successful.

CHAPTER 8:

False Assumptions About Owning a Small Business

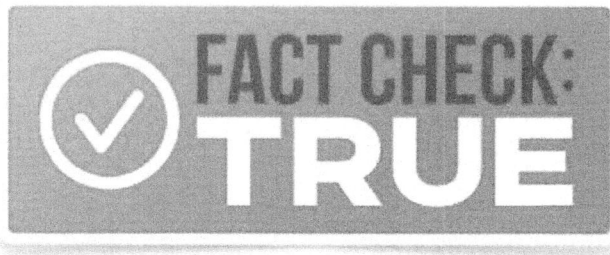

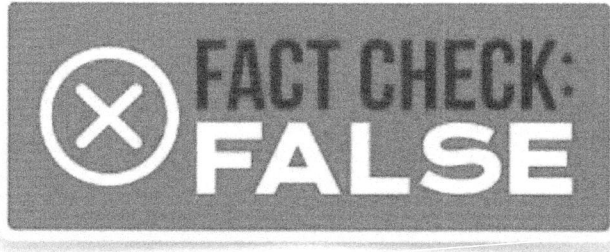

When individuals decide to start a small business or any business venture, most often, they start the process with assumptions ingrained in their brains about what the business environment would be like, without truly questioning what they hear or read. Having a belief without documented proof and research to back up that belief often leads the aspiring entrepreneur to make decisions and create strategies for their business that oftentimes is completely wrong for their business and they are left wondering what happened.

Some common false assumptions and strategies are:

MYTH #1: Relying on others for answers and information blindly

Do not believe everything you read and hear. Instead, get into the habit of researching information and knowledge you obtain from others and understand WHY and "**connect the dots**" between facts and concepts. If you do not know why situations and facts are the way they are, then you will not have the ability to critically think through every situation you will come across in the life span of your business. If you have a business and you find yourself unsure of what you should be doing, why people aren't buying or you are standing there twiddling your thumbs confused, then you either have done something wrong, do not talk to your customers enough to know what they need and want or you do not know enough about your business.

There is power in the knowledge YOU have and as a business owner, you should KNOW your business and all of the influencers around it. If you have control and knowledge about every facet of your business, you will know how to handle most if not all situations that happen within your business life span.

MYTH #2: There are free grants and banks that will loan individuals money if they are starting a business

This is not true. You will need to contribute capital out of your pocket to fund your business, EVEN if you are looking for funding from other sources. Lenders, for example, will expect you to contribute at least 15-20% of your funds (sometimes more than that) into the business or they will automatically assume that you have no faith in your business idea or that you do not have any financial responsibility or know-how.

Also, there are no truly **free grants** out there that will just give anyone funding. A few grants that do exist, are usually listed on www.grants.gov . These grants are usually geared towards educational institutions, nonprofits, specialized industries, or emerging technologies within industries **for a reason**.

If you are the type of person that would not hand over your money to a random stranger just because they are starting their business, do not assume others will. This includes financial institutions also. They too are doing business. They cannot stay afloat if they approved anyone walking through their doors asking for capital.

If you haven't found any grants you qualify for yet, it is because free grants for the general public typically do not exist and/or you do not meet the required stipulations provided by grants. Also, grants are never **free,** they always have stipulations attached and/or goals & requirements you have to achieve ahead of time before they fund your business.

MYTH #3: People will automatically love and know about your business when you officially launch

This is also not true. Remember, YOUR BUSINESS is the new entity that is coming into an already established marketplace. It is up to you to grab the attention of consumers who are already buying products/services that are similar to yours, from other businesses that are already in existence and convey to them in a way that they understand and like; that your business exists and has better value for them.

This isn't a **field of dreams** where if you build a business on a random street corner or create a website on the internet, that people will automatically know who you are. There are 14+ billion websites on the planet, for instance. How do you expect them to find you right away? It takes the proper marketing strategies and channels for them to hear about you and that takes time.

The more that you do pre-grand opening/launch marketing the more time you save when you do officially open.

MYTH #4: Being resistant to the notion that your original business idea and concept will change and evolve

Everyone who wants to start a business, typically falls in love with the concept that they want to start. So much so, that they are resistant to change any facet of it. The problem is consumers will only buy from a business if that business offers something that is a solution to their problems and needs.

Having a business isn't primarily about what YOU want, it is primarily about providing what potential customers want. Their purchases are what will be responsible for what hopefully keeps you in business. If you don't focus on their needs, wants, and preferences–they will not buy from you and you will not have the revenue to pay your expenses. At that point, you will no longer be in business.

You will need to put the customers first and their preferences change all the time. That is how trends and technology changes. As trends change, the marketplace you are in will change and your original business concept will have to evolve to keep in step with your changing industry. If you do not change with it, you will be left behind and will ultimately have to shut down your business.

MYTH #5: There is one set magic formula for everyone who wants to start a business

This is not true as well. Somewhere along the way in life, aspiring entrepreneurs grew up believing that there is some magical checklist in the sky that, if followed, their business will be successful. This is destructive thinking.

Although there are basic business principles and a basic flow, the start-up process for every single business, including ones in the same industry, **will be different.** There are **no** predesigned processes or timelines for your business because every business and vision within each business is different. The proper strategies and operations for your business all depend on what YOU want your business to look like and then you apply the basic principles to that.

Following a pre-designed checklist or any checklist will not make you successful, being aware of business principles, the influencers around and in your business, and having the proper strategies for your business are the **<u>minimum</u>** you will need to put your business on the right path.

These are just some of the false and risky assumptions that I see aspiring entrepreneurs and current business owners have every single day. Having these risky assumptions is what makes the business owners create strategies and decisions that negatively impact a business and they are left wondering where they went wrong.

The point of the five assumptions I listed above (and there are a lot more to this list) is that as the business owner, it is your responsibility to make the right decisions for your business and you cannot be a proper business owner if you are relying on anyone other than yourself to make your business successful. You have to plan ahead of time and take the logical steps to achieve the goals you want. You have to have patience and you have to think through every situation that you encounter. You have to make time for this.

CHAPTER 9:

How to Keep A Business Healthy in the Long Run

Surrounded in the least ambiguous terms, a business is a venture that gives an administration or an item to customers, in exchange for cash. Without customers, businesses would come up short. Furthermore, as an entrepreneur and proprietor of an online business, besides a reasonable pool of customers, you likewise need to have an impressive repertoire of hard and delicate aptitudes to see your business through good and bad times.

What Else Do You Need?

Times change and the components that started the seed of life for your business can change with them. Consider Kodak - the world leader in photographic film, it failed when it couldn't adjust rapidly enough to exploit the ascent of advanced imaging technology. The company reimagined itself and declared that it offered "bundling, useful printing, realistic interchanges and expert administrations for businesses around the globe," after coming up from the fiery debris of its previous success.

You need a long-term vision: where would you like to go with the business and where do you need it to take you?

What you likewise need for your business are good relationships. Strong relationships with your peers, accomplices, and partners in your business community are additionally imperative. Nobody ever really gets anywhere worth moving to, independent from anyone else. Help people, fabricate friendships, and your reward would be a supportive community, a profound feeling of belonging, and the benefit of having the option to give back.

To watch out for the health of your business, you need cozy information on what that means precisely.

What are your parameters for ideal health? In what key areas? What information do you need?

How would you track and accumulate the data you need? How far into the future would you be able to extrapolate from it?

What are your support plans in case of awful times, lean times, and crises?

What actions are you taking to forecast trends and search ahead for changes that will affect your business?

How Are You Preparing to Adjust So You Can Meet Those Trends?

There are things past your sphere of impact: what you can directly affect is the relationship you have with your customers, with your people, and with your peers. Concentrate on what you can change, construct substantial reserves to foresee and deal with the things you can't.

Customers and a flexible supporting workforce contribute directly to your bottom line and the survival of your business. Your test is to discover practical ways to enable them to be getting it done for whatever length of time that you need your business to last.

Any good business proprietor needs to be personally aware of the considerable number of things affecting the health of their business and for long term success to be assured, you are required to comprehend what you are dealing with to keep people interested in your items and relying on you. That means keeping up quality, support, and staying in contact with the need of the times.

Conceptualize gainful changes to stretch out beyond the bend. It resembles gaming in the future when you do this. Foresight as connected to industry trends and longer reaching shifts help you plan for the essential advancement of your business and avoid many changes. A piece of being successful is guaranteeing the strength of your business, which means having the option to navigate through harsh waters and make it out securely.

It's a presence of mind: to navigate well, you need to have a generally excellent idea of where the harsh patches would present themselves. If you can get a good idea where they would be simply the likeliest to give ahead of time, you can avoid them and if you can't locate some other way past them, you can prepare your business to withstand the inconvenience and the changes until you get clear.

Plan for The Most Exceedingly Terrible

Disaster planning is a piece of good business rehearses. This is where you dream up the most exceedingly terrible things that would possibly be able to happen to demolish your business and afterward, concoct ways to deal. You let your feelings of dread run wild, at that point when you have given them a chance to run down, you let rationale dominate.

Disaster-planning and prevention preparedness doesn't need to be done and completed all in a day. That would be genuinely debilitating and if you do choose to do this, enroll help from people who can offer firm support and understanding regarding what are the situations that may happen and to prompt you on those, so that you are ready to face them, when they occur.

Develop Solid Relationships

In case you missed reading between the lines, besides disaster planning, you likewise need a community of supportive, liberal people who you realize you can trust and rely on and that means developing solid, commonly gainful relationships crosswise over different social gatherings and assorted foundations. What you need to share for all intents and purposes is having the option to trust each other and respect what each brings to the table.

These sorts of relationships don't become medium-term. It requires investment and real exertion to developed stable connections, so you need to know about what you bring to the relationship and be happy to offer assistance notwithstanding when it doesn't appear to be required and prepare to finish if you don't have any desire to connect with people who take and don't give anything back, at that point, make an effort not to be one of those people. You can't get what you don't give, not in the long-term and we are talking long-term here, isn't that so?

Check-In, Assess, and Change as You Push Ahead

Set aside active squares time at regular interims to check in with your objectives, progress, and ventures. Similarly, as you can utilize every time on the weekend to plan and prepare for the week ahead, you can likewise use those times to assess the previous week and see what you can improve, adjust or drop in the week to come. Do this exercise, also for the end of the month and put those months in their place toward the end of one quarter to assess and plan forward to the next quarter.

CHAPTER 10:

How Do I Create Profitable and Predictable Processes

Before you can start building your predictable processes, you need to understand:

- Why you need them?

- What results you are looking to achieve?

- Who the processes should be created for?

- Where processes should be applied?

- How they will help you, your team, and your business growth?

- When do you need to create them?

Start with collecting data on all the tasks your team works on throughout the year. Then you can start formulating a plan of attack to build the necessary systems and processes.

Don't be afraid to question everything in your business. Going through this technique to find out what needs to be streamlined will likely ruffle feathers among your team, especially if they have been a part of your organization for a long time. Remind yourself constantly why you are going through the trouble of creating processes in the first place.

Start with just one operation at a time so you don't overwhelm yourself, your team, or your customers. I use the Five Ws to discover how I can best optimize the process needed:

- **Why** is the process needed?

- **What** are the desired results?

- **Who** is involved?

- **When and Where** is the process used?

- **How** will it affect the rest of my operation?

Answering the above questions will enable you to make informed conclusions before making an informed decision.
Now write out and number each step in the current method used to accomplish the specific task. Observe the current method taking place. Keep an eye out for all the inefficiencies happening because

you haven't been taking the time to ask, "Why?"

Once you have all the steps written, you should be able to see more clearly:

- How each step relates to the others?

- Which steps are unnecessary?

- Which steps can be completed together?

- How reducing steps will reduce costs and time?

- How advancing your technology could improve efficiency?

- Where adding steps could increase efficiency, quality control, and output?

Creating predictable processes is not always about conserving resources. In some cases, the increased output can be a big result of optimizing your processes by adding just a few extra steps.

Can You Franchise A Food Truck?

Most new food truck proprietors stroll into this industry with an entrepreneurial spirit, stirred due to and despite, the poor economy and all the more especially, the loss of a job. Given this downturn and despite it, we have seen a national ascent in the food truck industry.

When we think about the word 'entrepreneur', we regularly overlook that this word doesn't just imply people that have made business thoughts from scratch. Rather, entrepreneurs are business owners that have taken on types of risk that the vast majority are reluctant or incapable to effectively manage.

This definition opens up an entire course for aspiring food truck entrepreneurs to take on. Instead of making it necessary to suddenly become a brand-advertising expert, creative designer, or master chef, you may choose to turn into a food truck franchisee-which accompanies the greater part of the advantages of working in the food truck industry with less of the duty. It's ideal for people who have next to zero business foundation.

Let's take a look at a rundown of the pros and cons of joining a franchise:

Pros:

- There are fewer forthcoming decisions. Within a franchise, you are given instant brand acknowledgment. The menu, the name, and the design are given to you.

- You will have the expert help you need. The corporate office will provide you with help and staff that can address concerns and questions. This can be particularly useful for new business owners in the mobile food industry, as they may be new to how to manage issues that emerge.

- You have a name. What's more, with that name comes business. Your name is as of now known all through the city, state, and, sometimes, even the entire country.

Cons:

- Food truck franchisees need capital and loads of it. These endeavors can run up to $500,000 just to join them. What's more commonly that this price tag goes against the reason that business owners are looking to go into this industry in any case. All things considered, opening up a food truck should be a lot less expensive than running a physical café, right?

- The idea of the truck–name, design, and menu are given to you. Similarly, as this fills in as a pro for joining a franchise, it can likewise be viewed as a con. It takes into consideration little innovativeness, which is the thing that most business visionaries thrive on.

- You are paying royalties and other fees (relentless).

So, what will you choose? Keep up a receptive outlook and settle on key choices that are in line with your desires and personality. Opening any food truck business, regardless of whether it's a franchise or a truck from scratch is a long-haul choice that shouldn't be trifled with.

CHAPTER 11:

Food Truck Business Success Tips

Get Creative with Your Sauces

If you don't plan on serving foods that involve the traditional mustards and ketchup, you can ignore this one. However, for those of you who do, it's a good idea to put an extra effort into the staples to make them a bit more exciting.

Building on the example above, we used "double-smoked ketchup" and "ballpark mustard." The best way to follow through on these claims is to have a slightly more exciting ketchup or mustard. It doesn't take much effort to spruce these up a bit, and if you can add a bit of extra flavor to these, people will remember you for it.

Unless you are already familiar with how to do it, go online and check out how to make a good mayonnaise, or how to make your ketchup and mustard a bit more exciting. For my truck, we would mix a certain BBQ sauce with the ketchup, as well as something a bit spicy to make it a better tasting and more exciting ketchup. Mustard is great because there are so many different types of mustard that people rarely try. If you are not into making your own, check out what else is out there. A lot of people are in the dark when it comes to exotic mustard, and you can use this to your advantage by using a type they have never seen before.

*On a side note, it is still a good idea to have the classics there, as some people aren't interested in trying something new, and would prefer to stick with what they know.

As the weeks go by and you have more street days under your belt, you will want to keep track of how you are doing, so let's look at how best to do that...

Plan the Work, Work the Plan

Owning a food truck business can be a standout amongst the most agreeable of all businesses in the world. Consider it! Bolstering hungry individuals delicious, crisply cooked, heavenly suppers at costs you'd pay at the neighborhood greasy spoon. Be that as it may, before getting into this business, you must do some planning and thinking to make sense of, if you have the stuff to be successful. As with getting into any business, numerous components need to be considered. At the base of every one of these contemplations is the issue: "Would you say you are ready to work for yourself?"

You will be forceful, straightforward, and arranged to work your plan carefully before you can like to make progress. More food trucks are hitting the lanes regularly, and it must be your primary goal to guarantee your place among them and eventually ascend over the competition.

First, find out who and where the competition is? Make a rundown of the considerable number of cooking styles and choose what you can serve that will be unique and generally welcomed in your commercial center. Everything from your logo, truck structure to your decision on what to cook, in short, everything about your business must be unique. Of course, you will be sorted out when you are well organized, cognizant, and eco inviting.

Investigate to some degree every day, regardless of whether this situation energizes you or alarms you half to death, this may decide if you are up to be a gourmet food truck owner/administrator or not.

At 5:00 a.m., rise and sparkle. In a couple of hours, most of the world will be awake and every one of them hungry. You need to plan to bolster them.

At 5:30 a.m., stock up at the supermarket for crisp fixings (this could have been done the previous night if you have a POS framework).

At 6:00 a.m., drive to your assigned prep-kitchen, where you will meet your staff, and start getting ready food for the truck. For instance, cutting vegetables, apportioning the dish divides, preparing your extraordinary sauces, and so on.

At 8:30 a.m. till night (or at whatever point you make your dollar objective): serve that tasty food off your truck.

At 10:00 p.m., clean up and prepare for another group buster day tomorrow.

You will need some food information, imagination, media aptitudes, and showcasing abilities, except if you go with one of the establishment food truck organizations around. Complete a search for 'food truck establishments'. Perseverance is the name of the game. You need to be sharp when leading your research alone on the food truck business, as there are numerous guidelines relating to food trucks that contrast dependence on every city. Check with the regional branch of your nearby specialist for its specific instructions.

Trucks are mechanical, so you will need to line up a dependable and responsive repairer. This is very important. Concerning the appliances that accompany your truck, it is not a smart thought to purchase utilized, for you will never know how the past owner thought about the same thing. When they are new, these appliances are secured under their producers' guarantees. When you have purchased utilized appliances like a refrigerator, stovetop, and grill, they will by all means require an up-keep.

Concerning the bookkeeping, contracting a bookkeeper to deal with your business might be somewhat ridiculously cost shrewd, so consider somebody who knows QuickBooks or some other bookkeeping software programs. An attorney might be essential to work out the grant and stopping license, once more, there might be administrations out there that could help with this. You can also complete a search on Google.

Promoting? Indeed, this is very important. I feel compelled to press on the significance of web-based social networking as much as possible. No food truck has ever been successful without contacting the general society. The most prosperous food trucks use versatile applications, Twitter, and Facebook, among others. Keep in contact with clients, keep them near you as much as could be expected because this is another key to a successful business. Furthermore, if you need your client to know where you will be, complete a search on Food Truck versatile applications and see what's out there!

Not all food trucks owners maintain their full business time. A few trucks work just at the end of the week or after work hours. Full-time tasks, in the right area, will round up more money, yet on the other side; it requires a lot of effort. Whichever way you pick dependably keep a week after week schedule with set occasions for dealing with bills, covering government expenses, and of course for spreading the expression of your business online and among companions.

In the wake of mulling over and settling on a course of activity for your truck, record it, make a business plan that will enable you to accomplish your objectives quicker, and all the more proficiently.

What's more, a reasonable business plan is essential if you need to request loans from companions or the bank. Here as well, if you need loans, search online for Food Truck SBA loans. Everybody needs to see that their money is heading off to a possible money-production attempt, so the more exhaustive you are in setting up this business; the more successful you will be in persuading others to help.

Tracking Your Progress

Keep Track of What You Sell

It will be important that for the many days you spend at a certain spot or event, a track of what you have been selling has to be kept. This means keeping track of how many of each of the items were sold. This is important for several reasons.

For one, it lets you see what food items are selling best. If you regularly keep track of everything that has sold, you will probably begin to notice that some things sell very well each week, while others seem to be lagging. Keeping track of this also lets you know if prices should be changed, either to raise them or lower them.

This may seem obvious, but it is often easy to overlook. As the person coming up with the ideas and putting together the food for sale, it's often easy for judgment to be clouded.

You will probably be thinking that everything you are selling is a bestseller because you made it and it tastes good to you. But everyone is different, and asides from a few items, it is not always easy to predict just what people will like. So, do yourself a favor and keep track of the orders.

I generally do this by writing down on each order sheet what was ordered and for how much (along with the customer's name). I then save all of these slips of paper and review them after the day is done.

You don't need to get fancy and enter them into a spreadsheet. Just write down somewhere, how much of each item was sold, so that you can compare it to future service days to identify any trends in customer orders.

Keep Track of Your Costs

Selling food on the street can be more expensive than people realize. In addition to spending long hours prepping the food and making sure everything is set up for your street service day, you will be spending a fair amount of money on all the food, not to mention gas for your truck, a potential fee for the spot, etc. Costs can build up quickly even before you start selling.

A lot also depends on what type of day it is. If it's cold or raining, you could make a lot less than you originally expected, and a lot of that food could be wasted. Though these are the costs of operating a food truck, it will be important to keep track of these costs regularly. It's very easy, particularly if you are not very keen on the business side of things, to forget about expenses and pursue your goal of making amazing food recipes for people.

This is indeed crucial, but you don't want to go broke before you realize this dream. So, whether it's every service day, every week, or whatever you think is best, you should make sure to keep track of all your expenses regularly. There's nothing worse than looking at all your bills and costs after 6 months and realizing you lost a sizable amount of money.

Try to avoid this by monitoring costs regularly. This is most notable with the actual food. You may buy enough for a big crowd, only to get rained out and be left with a lot of food that goes into the garbage.

While no one can control the weather, you can plan for bad scenarios, so before you run off to buy 30 pounds of beef, consider the spot you will be serving at, how you've done in the past, and what problems might lead you to lose money. If in doubt, it's much more cost-efficient on the side of to purchase little food and sell-out, then be stuck with mountains of wasted food that cost you more than you can afford.

Keep Track of the Day's Revenue

This is worth mentioning for those who may forget to do so. You will want to make sure that you know your total sales for each day on the street. This will be important in deciding if your menu is on point, if the spot is worth it, and if you are advertising effectively. At the end of the day, the one thing that matters is how much money you are taking home after all expenses, and the best way to keep track of this is to track your sales day by day.

This way, you can match it against costs and see if you need to make a change or if what you are doing and where you are going seems to be working. It is an easy task and one that only requires a little bit of counting before and after.

Whatever bills and coins you bring, (and you should make sure you have enough) just keep track of the total you showed up with. At the end of the day, count the total amount of money, and subtract this initial amount, and you have your total sales. The other way to do it is to take your order slips with all the orders on it and add up the total from that. That will involve writing down a price on each order slip while you are taking the orders, but this is easy to remember once you do it a few times.

Take as Many Pictures as Possible

It's easy to forget to do this in the middle of a busy day, but this is exactly the time that you should be taking lots of pictures of people receiving food, people ordering, and above all lots of traffic around your truck. These are pictures you will use later for your website and social media accounts, and you want them to be full of customers.

Taking pictures of the truck is always cool because food trucks are cool. However, what drags people in is popularity. Nearly every street service day I've done, the truck that has the most people around it is the truck that makes the most money. This isn't necessarily just due to people hanging around out in front of the truck, but it does have a big influence on people who are unsure of what to get.

When people show up to eat and they have no prior knowledge of which trucks are good and which are average, they'll often go with the crowd and choose the one with the most people out front. When your truck gets busy, you will want to sneak out if possible and take some pictures. Taking pictures from outside where everyone is lined up and waiting is perfect.

The more people hanging about your truck, the more people will be drawn to it, and the more attention and hype you will get on social media. If people see pictures of a busy truck, they'll want to try it for themselves next time they can, so be sure to make a note of this, as it is easy to forget, and these opportunities don't come around often. Take advantage of the busy hours.

Have Pictures of Your Food Visible

If you have a high-quality camera, that's good for you but it's not essential. What you will want to do is have a blown-up picture of what you are serving somewhere close to where the description of the food on the menu is.

Make sure you've brought some tape. If you don't already have a picture of the food, you are serving that day then you will want to make up an order and take a picture of it, something you should do anyway. Print this off, make sure it's big enough, and take it with you.

Not every item is completely necessary, but your main items are important, and giving people a look at them, can go a long way to getting them to buy your food.

Make it a habit of taking a picture of every item you make. It's always a good idea to have a couple of different pictures of each item, or you will discover that you end up continually using the same picture on the same social media accounts, which is not very exciting.

In addition to these pictures, once you've made food for the day, take a picture of it and post it. That is exactly what people would expect to find that day at your truck. Along with a good description, this will be sure to attract lots of customers. The sky is indeed your limit, so post as many pictures as you feel like, but be sure to get pictures of all the items you will be serving up, on social media.

This is where it's important to have older pictures, as you might not have time to take a picture of each item on the day you are serving. Newer pictures are better but it's important just to have some pictures at hand so that you can quickly throw them up on your social media platforms if you don't have time to make up an order for picture purposes.

On a side note, when you are posting these pictures, don't bother putting how much it will cost. This may put some people off before they even get there. Instead, let them see what's being offered. Hopefully, this will draw them to your truck and by the time they've ordered, a couple of extra bucks won't matter to them as much anymore.

Let People Know Your Location

People need to know where to find you when you are out on the street. Since you are continually on the move, many people may not know your location. This is where you should be using social media to your advantage. Once you know your schedule for the week and where you will be, get it out on social media so that people will know what days you will be on the street and where you will be.

That way, people who like your food and want to have more of it will know well in advance where they can find you. It also means that people who like the food truck scene and want to try them out will know where they can find you. This will help bring in more people on the day of selling and will mean you won't just be relying on people walking by.

It is a good idea to constantly be updating this and reminding people where you will be. Doing it early in the week is a good idea, and it's also a good idea to do it periodically throughout the week. Make sure to do it the day before you head out. That way, people will have multiple chances to see where you are and will be reminded of it throughout the week and remember when you will be at a spot near them.

Prep as Much as Possible Before Arriving

There's nothing worse than seeing people showing up at your truck window ready to order food and you are still busy chopping onions. Some things may seem like they can be done in a little time that you will be able to squeeze a few of the smaller prep jobs in, before opening, but in almost all cases you will find out that you are pressed for time once you arrive.

It always takes a bit longer to set up than you think it will once you arrive, and adding on additional prep work that could be done before arriving isn't something that should be taking up this valuable time.

Arriving there early is important but do yourself a favor and take care of the smaller prep jobs before you arrive. That way, you can focus on what needs to be done at the service spot, as well as being able to relax before starting your cooking day.
Also, just because you may be opening at noon, people will often look to show up early to avoid any potential lines and you want to be ready to take their orders, especially if other trucks are still getting ready to open.

So be prepared, prep before you arrive, and take advantage of being open before the other trucks.

Test Your Food Before You Sell It

This is probably something you are already doing anyway, but if not it's an important step to remember, for a few reasons. No matter how many times you've made the item you will be selling, when it comes to the food you can never be certain how things will turn out. It could be that something is off with the meat or cheese, or that a certain sauce doesn't taste right.

In any event, it will be disastrous if you are serving food that isn't what you thought it would be, and bad food equals unhappy customers and no repeat business. So be sure to make a few test items either the night before or the day of your event or street service.

This also gives you the chance to take a picture and put it on Instagram and Twitter, with the bonus of you getting to eat and enjoying the fruits of your labor!

Have a Tip Jar

This often goes overlooked, but it shouldn't. Having a tip jar is an easy way to get a bit of extra cash out of the gig. As you will be serving on the street, and likely only taking cash, customers will generally have some extra change, either on hand or from the change you give them when they break a bill.

And, more so than a restaurant, people are generous with tips, it just seems to be a street thing. So be sure to have a tip jar out by the window. It's an easy way to earn some extra money, and people like giving tips, it makes it a good way to connect with your customer base. If your food is great, the next time they come back, they'll be even more willing to drop a few bucks in.

Just as a tip (bad pun), I'd recommend throwing a few bucks in at the beginning of the day. This makes it appear that people DO give tips, but it doesn't make it seem like you are cleaning up. Throw something funny or interesting like a quote on the outside of the jar so that it gets noticed.

Clean the Truck at The Day's End

This is one of those things that should be obvious, and indeed is a no-brainer for a lot of people, but for people like me, it is often something that requires a little more self-discipline than I usually have at the end of a long day. Let's face it, you've been up since the crack of dawn prepping and making sure everything is ready for the day. You've been on your feet all day cooking and serving food, and finally, you are driving that big, slow truck all the way home.

Ignoring this first chance to clean can be costly. For one, you can forget, and be ready to pull out for your next service only to find the truck a complete mess and not ready to use. It can also mean that food spills can harden, and the grill and other tabletops can be a mess.

This can also lead to flies and other unwanted parties happening in your truck, which can be a real headache to clean up, especially when the food is old and rotting. Do yourself a favor and clean the truck before you finally relax.

Conclusion

Lunch trucks have been in use for over 2 decades. The fundamental thought of the lunch truck is to serve food to individuals situated in various areas. The main lunch truck was invented way back in the nineteenth century for the military which served food to their officers. This was known as a mobile lunch service. They were served with coffee and snacks which were easy to make with the technology they had during their time. Presently, as technology has progressed and given us various equipment for kitchen use, the advanced lunch trucks carry all the vital and current amenities that are required in the kitchen.

Lunch trucks are known for their benefits. When contrasted and the stationary cafés, lunch trucks have indicated great profit and a great client base. If you can give the clients the great quality of food that they can afford, you can likewise expect a few loyal clients following in various areas that you intend to go around. As you would be moving from one spot to the others, you have the chance to serve more individuals and with various menu choices.

The underlying investment that you would make is on the vehicle. With numerous models accessible in the market, you should pick the one which will fill your need. Next would be the equipment that you require, for example, the stainless-steel sinks, oven, fridge, and other embellishments, for example, the cutlery sets, plates, and so forth before you start off with your new business, there are scarcely any rules that you need to follow. With the government presenting stringent guidelines for mobile food services, it is fundamental for you to keep every one of the principles to remain in the business.

You are likewise required to get the mobile food service permit from the legislature before kicking-off your business. You can go to the local government authorities who will help you with respect to the license details. The modern lunch trucks are furnished with current sterile solutions to keeping the environment and the earth clean; giving a hygienic atmosphere for the clients to eat their food.

If you can't invest in the underlying amount that is required for obtaining the vehicle and also the important embellishments for the kitchen, you can then approach a franchise from where you can purchase his food items. When you secure a deal with a franchise, they will give all of you the important equipment for the kitchen and the lunch truck. The main thing that you have to do is to head to various areas and serve the food. Regardless of the path you pick, mobile food service permit is a must.

If you might want to expand the benefits to the following level, present additional services that will satisfy the clients and at the same time increases the client base as well as the loyal customer following. Aside from the lunch boxes that you provide, you can likewise present ice creams and desserts on the menu.

The food truck business, though, is not a smooth sail for everyone. There are going to be a number of hurdles in your business encounters that I did not cover in this book. I've tried to cover all the fundamentals but naturally, I can't prepare you for everything. All I hope is, every now and then as you build your business, you think to yourself, "Hey, that was a good idea!" from something you read in this book.

May your difficulties be few and sales are many!

Made in the USA
Las Vegas, NV
06 September 2021